THE MAKING OF

Waterworld *Titles from Boulevard Books*

———————

WATERWORLD
A NOVEL BY MAX ALLEN COLLINS

WATERWORLD
A YOUNG ADULT NOVEL BY MAX ALLEN COLLINS

THE MAKING OF WATERWORLD
BY JANINE POURROY

———————

THE MAKING OF

WATERWORLD

By Janine Pourroy

BOULEVARD BOOKS, NEW YORK

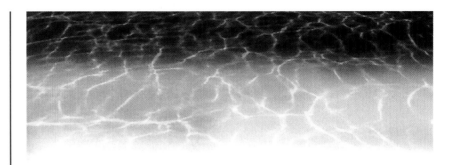

Grateful acknowlegment is made to the following for their contributions to this book:

All costume sketches by John Bloomfield
All photos from set by Ben Glass
Storyboard sequences by Steve Burg
Sketches of weapons by Stefan Dechant
Sketches of vehicles by Stefan Dechant

Book Design by H. Roberts Design

This is an original edition from The Berkley Publishing Group
and has never been previously published.

THE MAKING OF WATERWORLD
A Boulevard Book / published by arrangement with
MCA Publishing Rights, a Division of MCA, Inc.

PRINTING HISTORY
Boulevard trade edition / August 1995

ISBN: 1-57297-005-7

BOULEVARD
Boulevard Books are published by The Berkley Publishing Group
200 Madison Avenue, New York, New York 10016.
BOULEVARD and its logo are trademarks
belonging to Berkley Publishing Corporation.

PRINTED IN THE UNITED STATES OF AMERICA

10 9 8 7 6 5 4 3 2 1

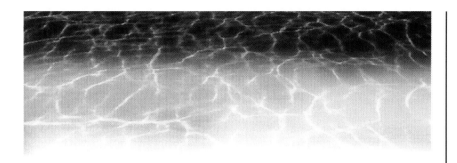

Acknowledgments

Like the story itself, making *Waterworld* was, indeed, a quest,

and I would like to thank the filmmakers, cast and crew

for sharing the account of their journey with me — frequently in the midst

of an extraordinarily demanding production schedule.

Thanks also to Nancy Cushing-Jones of MCA Publishing for the

opportunity to participate in this project and to Debra Mostow,

Karen Davis and Carolyn McCue for assistance and liaison.

Further gratitude must be expressed to Don Shay and Jody Duncan,

for their years of friendship and support—

and for making all things possible.

My final thanks go to my children, Jessie and Trevor,

and to my husband, Jim, for being, quite simply the best.

Janine Pourroy

THE MAKING OF

WATERWORLD

1. THE QUEST

If you could see it all, before you go—
all the adversity you face at sea—
you would stay here, and guard this house, and be immortal.

Homer

It is a challenge as ancient as the sea itself. The idea of capturing, in some way, the power and mystery of the earth's vast waters has compelled humankind from the beginning of time. We cannot escape its pull; we are as bound to the ocean as it is to the moon, whose shining face calls forth the monthly tide. It is a yearning the Greek writer Homer understood very well when he chronicled the exploits of brave Ulysses in his epic poem *The Odyssey*. The hero's quest was not a tale of dusty battlefields and landlocked foe; it was a fabulous story born of the sea.

The appeal of conquering the ocean has not diminished much in the past 3,500 years. Fascination with the sea has remained consistently compelling for mariners and storytellers alike. For cinematic storytellers, however, the formidable task of making a viable movie filmed almost exclusively on water has been approached with caution, and with good reason. Shooting on water is one of the most daunting challenges a filmmaker can face. Water is inconstant; it moves and changes form from one moment to the next. The lighting challenges are innumerable, and the attendant weather concerns make adhering to a production schedule trying at best. Many movies have been made about the sea, and many have filmed extensively there, but the notion of constructing full-size sets and filming them almost *entirely* on water had heretofore been considered an impossibility.

Then came *Waterworld,* and for director

Kevin Reynolds, actor/producer Kevin Costner, and producer Charles Gordon, the impossibility became a challenge to accomplish something no one had ever done before: to create a futuristic world that was built completely on water.

Reynolds and Costner had first paired up for the 1985 release *Fandango* and formed an immediate and lasting friendship. They worked together again on *Robin Hood: Prince of Thieves* in 1991, but had no specific plans to collaborate on another project when *Waterworld* came to their attention. "Kevin and I have always traded material," noted Reynolds. "We both seem to like the same kinds of pieces. I had come across an early draft of *Waterworld* in 1988 and really liked it, so I showed it to Kevin and he liked it, too. I didn't think about it for a while and we were both busy with other projects when, unbeknownst to one another, we simultaneously approached the Gordons, who had bought the script on speculation for Largo Entertainment. I had been toying around with what I was going to do next when I called Larry and said, 'Do you still have that *Waterworld* script? Are you doing anything with it?' So I came in and had a meeting with him and he said, 'Guess who else wants to do it?'"

For Costner, *Waterworld* offered an opportunity to try his hand at a genre unlike any he had previously encountered. "I'm always looking for a fresh experience in the theater," he said. "I take my family to the movies just like everybody else, and I watch the previews that play beforehand. They really give you a feeling about whether or not you want to see a particular movie. I thought about the exotic quality of *Waterworld*—and that it is a real action-adventure—and it reminded me of what it is I like about movies. I personally don't do straight dramas or comedies or love stories; I also haven't done a sequel. *Waterworld* was an opportunity to make a movie like I had never made before, and I think it fit very well into the same scheme as doing something unusual like *Field of Dreams* or *Dances with Wolves*." *Waterworld* provided the friends with an opportunity to reinstate a working relationship while offering an intriguing cinematic challenge.

The script had originated with a young writer named Peter Rader, who came to Los Angeles in 1983 after graduating from Harvard. Long interested in being a part of the movie business, Rader worked the gamut of below-the-line production jobs while waiting for the opportunity to participate in the more creative areas of writing and directing. By 1986 he was ready to get a low-budget feature off the ground when he met with Brad Krevoy, who was then Roger Corman's right-hand man at New Horizons. Corman's production company had long been known for giving young talent the opportunity to write and direct under low-budget circumstances. "Brad knew I wanted to direct," Rader recalled, "and he told me that if I would write a *Mad Max* rip-off, he would arrange financing and I could have a hand at directing. I went home and thought about it and decided that I didn't want to do another *Mad Max* rip-off. It seemed like everyone was doing

> "I thought about the exotic quality of Waterworld—and that it is a real action-adventure—and it reminded me of what it is I like about movies," Costner said.

them—it was the classic low-budget thing to do. I wondered, 'What if we set the whole thing on water? I went back and pitched it to him and he took one look at me and said, 'Are you out of your mind? It would cost us three million dollars to make that movie.'"

Although the initial negotiations for *Waterworld* came to an abrupt end, Rader remained fascinated with the idea. He decided to proceed with a script, but this time approached it from an entirely different angle. Instead of writing around low-budget film restrictions such as modest locations and available resources, Rader decided to write the most outrageous story he could come up with. "I started thinking in a completely different way," he said. "I thought about what *I* wanted to see on the screen, about what would be the most visually staggering and incredible. I thought about writing an epic no one had ever seen before."

Rader began by making a daily excursion across town to borrow his cousin's computer. "I was so broke at that time I didn't even own a computer," he admitted. "My cousin was very supportive of me and let me use her Macintosh to write the script. She also happened to be a line producer who had connections with Larry Gordon, so when I finished it, I gave it to her to read. She said, 'This would be perfect for Larry Gordon. Do you want me to give it to him?' But I was kind of shy at the time and didn't pursue it. I *did*, however, give it to the only writer I knew at that point—my cousin's friend who was a working screenwriter—and he absolutely trashed it. He *really* hated it. I was so mortified that I just put it on the shelf for three years."

Preproduction preparations for the film included creating meticulous storyboards of each action sequence.

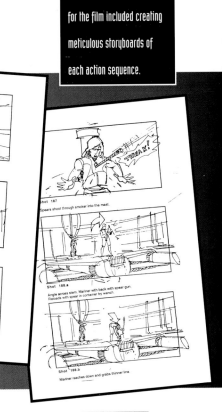

The atoll was central to setting the look for the production.

During that three-year period Rader ended up directing a couple of low-budget features for a Greek production company—a harrowing experience that left him completely disenchanted with the entire B movie genre. "I became so disillusioned with that path of the movie business that I decided I wouldn't do any more films of that nature," he said. "I even thought about getting out of the business entirely. So while I was considering my options, I dusted off my old *Waterworld* script and I thought, 'You know, this isn't bad. It's actually kind of good.' I spent a month doing a rewrite and then started circulating the revised draft among some of the new contacts I'd made over the years."

Among Rader's new contacts were Andy Licht and Jeff Mueller, who read the reworked *Waterworld* script and loved it. Licht and Mueller had produced a couple of teen comedies called *License to Drive* and *Little Monsters* and were eager to try their hand at a completely different genre. *Waterworld* provided them with the opportunity they'd been looking for. "We initially liked that it was an action-adventure story that took place on water," recalled Mueller. "That was really something different. We also liked that it was about creating a new world, which was a unique opportunity—there aren't many movies that do that. The third thing about *Waterworld* was that it seemed like another way of doing a Western without doing a Western—sort of a Sergio Leone vision of the mysterious drifter who becomes a reluctant hero."

Rader's reluctant hero was called Noah, a sea-hardened loner who kept a white stallion on board his large, customized river barge. His images were at once epic and fantastic, and drew on both mythical and biblical allusions. The heroine was a strong and beautiful woman named Helen, after Helen of Troy. Noah's nemesis was the pirate leader Neptune, a large, ruthless man with a long, pointed beard who carried a forked staff. Neptune surrounded himself with mutant henchmen such as the shark-toothed Orca, and a crustacean-armed character called Lobster. Helen's young charge, Enola—the child who would lead her people to land—was found, like Moses, adrift and surrounded by branches. Rader had given Enola her name for two compelling reasons: the *Enola Gay* was the bomber that dropped atomic destruction on Hiroshima in 1945, and Enola spelled backward is "Alone." The denizens of Waterworld lived on a floating artificial island called Oasis and dreamed of a legendary land called Ararat— named for Mt. Ararat, the highest mountain in Turkey where Noah's Ark purportedly came to rest after the biblical deluge.

Licht began by helping Rader find an agent; then he and Mueller approached John Davis, with whom they had a producing agreement. In an ironic turn, Davis took *Waterworld* to Larry Gordon, the producer Peter Rader had been too shy to bother a few years earlier. "At Largo, the first obstacle I had to face was Larry Gordon," admitted Davis. "I'd been pitching the script around town and several studios were interested, but they were also afraid because it was such a big movie. When I went to Larry's office to convince him to buy this piece of material he decided that *Waterworld* offered the kind of cinematic possibilities he was looking for. The deal was signed on Christmas Eve 1989."

Rader had begun a series of script revisions with Licht and Mueller, and continued making adjustments with Davis and the people at Largo, including Lloyd Levin who was then president of the company. His original vision of *Waterworld* had been based on postapocalyptic destruction— nuclear war had melted the polar ice caps causing a global deluge. The story evolved to reflect a more environmental slant. Instead of nuclear war, the polar ice caps had melted as a result of global warming. Various characters and plot points were developed as well, with Rader completing a total of seven drafts for what was intended to be a Largo production. Meanwhile, Larry Gordon's partner, JVC, having decided *Waterworld* had become too big a project for Largo to produce alone, presented it to Universal Pictures, where they had a distribution deal. Finally, in December 1992—six years after Rader had pecked out his original script on a borrowed computer—a deal was made with Universal to produce the film.

Earlier that year, Kevin Costner called his friend Charles Gordon and said, "What's this *Waterworld* thing?" Gordon had made it a practice to keep Costner apprised of new material ever since the Gordon brothers had produced the much-acclaimed *Field of Dreams* in 1989.

"So I sent him the script," recalled Gordon, "and the next thing I knew,

"Rader had given Enola her name for two compelling reasons: the Enola Gay was the bomber that [destroyed] Hiroshima in 1945, and Enola spelled backward is 'Alone.'"

he called me back and said he loved it and wanted to do it with me producing and Kevin Reynolds directing." Gordon was understandably pleased to produce what had become a Kevin Costner/Kevin Reynolds film and was eager to get started. A veteran of such action-adventure movies as *The Rocketeer* and *Die Hard*, he appreciated the fact that *Waterworld* wasn't typical of the genre. "*Waterworld* was something that had never been done before," he noted, "and that was exciting. When you make movies you're always looking for something different, and I loved the fact that this was something no one had ever done. People said to me, 'Shoot this movie on *water*? Are you *crazy*? Don't you know what they say about shooting on water?' To me, that was a challenge. We had the same kind of reaction when we did *Field of Dreams*. 'A movie about ghosts, farming, and baseball? You're going to do a movie about those three ideas?' And we said, 'Yeah.' And pulled it off."

*   *   *

With Universal's backing and the involvement of both Kevin Costner and Kevin Reynolds solidified, the project took a decidedly different turn. The filmmakers began considering their vision for *Waterworld* and started developing story ideas and artistic concepts of their own. Writer R. J. Stewart was hired to try his hand at a new draft that would reflect some of those conceptual changes. A skilled illustrator was also needed to help visualize the strange new world they were creating. Costner immediately thought of Steve Burg, a storyboard artist with whom he had worked on *Dances with Wolves*. Costner recalled that Burg had considerable experience creating unusual realities—having worked on *The Abyss, Total Recall,* and *Terminator 2*—and that he had also worked as a conceptual artist. Burg was hired as an illustrator and in January 1993 set up shop in a trailer at Tig Productions—Kevin Costner's production company named after his grandmother—located on the Warner Brothers lot.

During this early conceptual design phase, Kevin Reynolds headed for Easter Island—a remote location in the South Pacific some 2,000 miles from the nearest mainland—to film *Rapa Nui,* a project he had spent a number of years initiating and preparing for. Burg began to develop the look of the movie based on a seven-page story outline the director had drafted before he left. Working along with Kevin Costner and Charles Gordon, Burg's first task was to come up with a "hero boat" for the lead character. "I knew nothing about boats," admitted Burg. "So the first thing I did was research. We knew we wanted it to be a very unique craft and we discussed building a catamaran, which is a sailboat that has two parallel hulls. In the course of doing my research, however, I became very interested in trimarans—which have three hulls—because they had more interesting possibilities. The first thing I did was draw a trimaran and a catamaran, both with the same treatment and said, 'What do you think?' Everybody agreed that the trimaran was much more intriguing." The judgment was both aesthetic and practical: in addition to being visually appealing, the trimaran also offered the most stable sailboat design available.

It was known from the start that the hero of *Waterworld* was a loner who lived a completely self-sufficient existence on his unique, highly customized craft. The idea for the boat was almost out of *The Swiss Family Robinson*—counterweights would cause the hero to fly up to the top of the mast; cranes and rigs set at multiple control stations would provide for every conceivable need. An early concept rendering showed a vessel so covered with planks and gadgets that it was almost unrecognizable as a boat. Scaffolding ran up to the top,

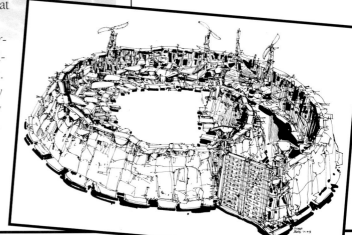

Two early versions of the atoll, including the nautilus entrance spiral.

with plants in containers growing along the back. A small house, reminiscent of a grass hut, was erected on the deck. It was a vision of a scavenged existence at its most inventive.

It was also known from the beginning that the hero would sail into some kind of colony at sea. Called the Oasis, it started out as several boats tied together, forming a circle of survival. The thinking was that over hundreds of years more and more boats had joined the city, which became increasingly larger in scale and population. The citizens of such a place would use whatever materials they could find—such as floating plastics or fiberglass—to reconfigure their home and transform it into new structures. The circular formation would be built around a central harbor or lake, and was somewhat reminiscent of the old wagon train idea, where early settlers joined together to create an immediate, 360-degree fortification in the wide-open plains of pioneer days. Burg also knew that part of the Oasis would include an Organo Barge—a section intended for composting and processing organic material, including dead bodies—as well as a prison, a school, and a tavern. Another early element of the script had to do with the pirates, who consumed vast amounts of fossil fuel and sought out isolated oases to pillage and plunder. A derelict oil tanker called the *'Deez* loomed somewhere in the fog as the dark side's version of Ararat, while the pirates lived in a watery camp made of boats. Burg continued to chip away at design concepts with Costner and Gordon—while maintaining cumbersome contact with Reynolds who was on location a world away—until Costner left to begin work on *A Perfect World.*

Prior to Burg's hiring, Charles Gordon had contacted another *Field of Dreams* alumnus, Dennis Gassner, who had served as production designer for the project. Gassner had gone on to win an Academy Award for his efforts on *Bugsy* in 1991 and was still heavily involved with *The Hudsucker Proxy* when Gordon asked him about designing the look for *Waterworld.* Gassner found the project interesting, but had to decline because of his commitment to *Hudsucker.* Months later, however, Gassner had long since completed the project and found himself at a loss. "I finished *Hudsucker* and was actually starting to look for another show," he recalled. "I couldn't find anything I *really* wanted to do. I read about twenty scripts and nothing especially appealed to me.

"Then I remembered *Waterworld* and gave Chuck a call. I asked him if he'd finished the movie and he said, 'No, we've barely started. I still haven't found anybody to do the production design.' He sent me a script and I thought it was fabulous." Gassner had an initial, long-distance phone conversation with Kevin Reynolds, and then made a four-day excursion to Easter Island to meet with the director in person. By May, a working agreement was reached and Gassner returned to Los Angeles to begin his involvement with *Waterworld.*

Gassner's first task was to define a reality for the new world they were creating. What would life *really* be like for a society of survivors bounded by an infinite ocean? Gassner's solution was simple: apply pure logic. "The only way you can approach a project like this is with pure logic," he noted. "We needed to establish a look for a futuristic period of time in a world made entirely of water. The date was 2500—what would things look like in that year? Then the analysis started to take place. We knew that plastic was going to end up being involved because wood products—in most cases—would start to break down. So in planning the city, we understood

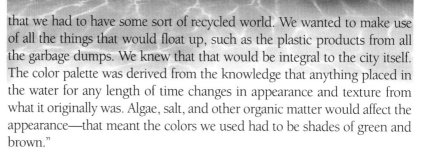

that we had to have some sort of recycled world. We wanted to make use of all the things that would float up, such as the plastic products from all the garbage dumps. We knew that that would be integral to the city itself. The color palette was derived from the knowledge that anything placed in the water for any length of time changes in appearance and texture from what it originally was. Algae, salt, and other organic matter would affect the appearance—that meant the colors we used had to be shades of green and brown."

Finding a location for the film was another preproduction essential. Gassner put together an itinerary of all the places where he thought the movie could be made and then went on a twenty-four-day, eighteen-airplane journey around the world seeking the ideal location. He started with the Kona Coast of the Big Island of Hawaii—a location noteworthy for its stunning blue water and isolation, coupled with reasonable access to supplies and lodging. He then went through Japan and Hong Kong, with a particular interest in observing Hong Kong Harbor and its bustle of humanity living and functioning on a world of boats. The Great Barrier Reef in Australia was visited along with Malta—an island in the Mediterranean south of Sicily— and then the Bahamas and Florida. Ultimately, however, the decision was made to film at the first location Gassner had visited—the Big Island of Hawaii, settling specifically on the Port of Kawaihae. "Kawaihae Harbor provided all the things none of the other locations provided," said Gassner. "It provided a warehouse—an old sugar shack, really—that could be used as studio space for interior sets. And the harbor was great—the boat commissioner, Ronald Black, was wonderful and helped work things out for us. Besides that, the water was uniquely beautiful, like nothing we'd ever seen."

Another design consideration involved building the set—now called the atoll because of its circular configuration—as a full-scale floating city rather than attempting to construct and film a miniature set. The decision, once again, was based on logic. "There was live action in too many situations for us to have done this as a miniature," explained Gassner. "It simply wasn't practical. The size was too big for a stage. We needed to sail the hero's boat through gates and have it come in, park, back up, and turn around. Kevin Reynolds also planned a number of battle sequences to take place there. So we worked with models and sketches and showed them to the producers. Everybody understood that a full-size set was what was physically needed."

Once again, the Kawaihae Harbor location proved ideal. It would be possible to set the full-scale atoll in the water and position it to reveal only open sea behind it. It could then be rotated to facilitate various camera angles. Later on, it could be towed all the way out to open sea.

With a location set, the fledgling art department—which had relocated to a trailer on the Universal lot—continued to refine the look of the film. The staff had expanded to include art director David Klassen and illustra-

"There was live action in too many situations for us to have done this [atoll] as a miniature. It simply wasn't practical."

tor Stefan Dechant, who worked alongside Burg and Gassner in developing a look for *Waterworld*. Their most immediate concerns were with the trimaran and atoll. Designs for the two were inseparable. The size of the trimaran dictated the size and scope of the atoll because of the significant amount of action to be set within its gates—and the dimensions of the trimaran had been determined almost from the beginning of the design phase. While doing research earlier in the year, Burg had looked through a sailing magazine and come across a racing boat by a French company called Jeanneau. It seemed possible to obtain a contemporary boat that offered state-of-the-art technology while providing a suitable foundation for the modifications called for in the script. Besides that, Gassner and everyone else agreed that the trimaran was an absolutely stunning piece of work. The French racing single-hander was the fastest of its class in the world. Intended for transatlantic open-ocean racing, it was at once powerful and exotic. As soon as the filmmakers saw the sailing machine in action, they were enthralled. Moreover, Jeanneau was equally intrigued with the *Waterworld* project and agreed to collaborate in the trimaran's design and construction. It was clear that the sailboat from Jeanneau was the perfect hero boat.

Burg had originally been working on designs for a futuristic-looking craft that would be aged to seem centuries old for the movie—sort of the *Millennium Falcon* idea from *Star Wars*. Instead of the earlier river barge concept, the notion of a boat that could transform from a clunky, utilitarian trawling mode into a sleek, high-powered escape mode had evolved. The Mariner, as the hero character was now called, required a vessel that could be handled by one person, while being equipped to manage such a transformation. The logic was that the Mariner had spent a lifetime on this boat and had customized it to serve every conceivable need. It was equipped with such essentials as a urine purifier, a harpoon gun and other weapons, along with various other gadgets that included a solar-powered hot glue gun for repairs. An eggbeater-style windmill spun drowsily in the wind, dredging up potential treasure from the ocean floor below. It was the perfect survival craft in every way. At the first sign of danger the Mariner could instantly transform his waterborne homestead into a no-nonsense racing craft. The designs were now adjusted to suit the parameters of the sixty-by-forty-five foot French trimaran, which would be modified and dressed to suit the reality of Waterworld.

During this conceptual phase, another writer had been hired to renovate the script once more. R. J. Stewart's draft hadn't quite been what Kevin Reynolds was looking for and David Twohy was brought on board to give it a try. The story evolved and changed into a less fantastic, more realistic vision. Aside from transforming the Noah character into the Mariner—a stranger without a name—the white horse of earlier drafts disappeared. In a way, the trimaran had replaced the hero's noble steed. There were no more mutant villains tagging alongside their pirate leader. The archvillain was now called the Deacon and his followers were made up of an oily, rag-tag group of miscreants known as Smokers. A new character named Old Gregor was introduced as a kind of visionary/inventor who lived in a special windmill-topped tower. The atoll shifted from a city of boats strung together to an impressive construct erected from recycled plastic, and the *'Deez* was no longer a mysterious Mecca for the bad guys, it was their home.

From his remote location, Kevin Reynolds kept in touch with the design department via telephone and Federal Express. Divergent time zones and air flights that arrived on the island only twice weekly made communication awkward at best. Although deeply entrenched in the day-to-day logistical problems of shooting *Rapa Nui*, Reynolds managed to convey to Gassner his overall vision for *Waterworld*. "I always knew what I wanted the philosophy of the picture to be," the director remarked, "and I used the creativity of Dennis Gassner and the design department to interpret that for me. That's always what you do as a filmmaker—you allow the different departments to take your vision and interpolate it through their own creativity. I wanted *Waterworld* to look epic, very epic, and not cartoonish at all. Being an environmentalist, I also liked the notion that the story was about a world that was flooded and there was no more dry land—that this is what could happen to us if we don't take care of our planet. *Waterworld* is an action-adventure picture, and it's meant to entertain, but I still liked the idea of trying to slip a message in. I wanted to pit two conflicting philosophies against each other: the Atoller/Mariner good guy philosophy being that you have to appreciate the world and what it is and take care of it, and the Smoker/Deacon bad guy philosophy, which is how do we get more, and use it all up, and there will always be another place to pillage."

Reynolds saw the Atollers as practical people who had learned to make do with virtually every scrap they could find. "Everything is derivative in Waterworld," he observed. "The people have no more resources, so everything is patched-together remnants of what was. Hopefully, it is still apparent that those remnants are elements of our present-day world—only centuries removed. I thought of it as one of those graphic representations of something that's been divided up into grids; then imagined what would happen if one was to start pulling away pieces of that grid until there's barely enough of the original picture left to recognize what it was in the first place. I wanted Waterworld to be like that grid, so that we could barely recognize what it once was—but see that some way or another it *was* something we know today. It was supposed to be centuries in the future, but I wanted it always to be couched somehow in our world."

Although considerable conceptual work and planning had been accomplished by this point, the preproduction phase officially began in September 1993. The reality of *Waterworld* had been established, and Gassner and crew could now concentrate on getting the design and construction of the trimaran under way. Under normal circumstances, Jeanneau required at least a year to build a single trimaran. The problem was, *Waterworld* required *two* highly specialized vessels—one for the trawling mode, which would be rigged for the transformation, and the other to serve in the escape mode capacity—and it needed them to accommodate a rapidly approaching first-unit shooting schedule. Instead of one year to build one boat, Jeanneau agreed to build two in an unprecedented five-month period of time. They began the design work in early September. To assist with the complicated transformation effect, Gassner called on mechanical-effects designer Peter Chesney, with whom he had worked on both *Miller's Crossing* and *The Hudsucker Proxy*. Gassner knew that Chesney's nautical background and engineering expertise would make him an asset on the multifaceted project.

Gassner and Chesney traveled to France to work with Jeanneau in determining how the boat was going to operate relative to the film. Aside from working out how the actual transformation from trawling to escape mode would be accomplished, it was also necessary to figure out a way to maneuver the craft *without* Kevin Costner having to steer and perform at the same time. "Trimarans aren't really boats," commented Chesney, "they're machines—and piloting such a craft is extremely difficult, even for an experienced sailor. We knew Kevin was going to have his hands full with his performance as the Mariner, so we had to come up with a plan for the boat to be steered in another way. It was clear that we could not put a crew on the deck; fast passes and helicopter shots would have revealed that the Mariner was not alone. We had to figure out a way to control the sails and steering and communication from inside the hulls—which was a huge task." Chesney worked with Jeanneau's naval architect Bruno Belmont in equipping the trimarans with a complex internal operating system.

To assist in visualizing the dynamic trimaran transformation, Gassner asked Stefan Dechant to create a three-dimensional computer animation showing the effect. Dechant had performed a similar duty on *Jurassic Park*, where he used a computerized Video Toaster effects system to construct and animate a three-dimensional tyrannosaur. The effect was quickly produced and helped establish motion and pacing for the animation personnel on that film. Gassner knew a similar effect was essential to visualize the trimaran transformation, as well as to work out the potential problems not readily apparent in the two-dimensional illustrations. "Steve Burg had done a series of rough sketches showing the transformation," explained Dechant, "and we really had a feeling about the way this thing would work. But you can cheat in a drawing and not even know it—and with the trimaran we had to be sure. It's only when you're dealing with something in 3-D that you start to understand how it's *really* going to happen. It was a long process of trying to solve the problems involved—knowing how the mast would snap together, for example, and where the blades would go and what the counterweights would do—and it took about four weeks to complete. By that time we had a nice little animation we were able to drop down on tape. Besides showing the designers how it would work, it was a good way to communicate with Kevin Reynolds, who was still on Easter Island, and with Kevin Costner, who was now working on *Wyatt Earp*—as well as with Charles Gordon.

"From that base, we added some simple animations of a figure symbolizing the Mariner, which moved through the routine of hitting the switches and mechanisms that caused the boat to transform. It gave us a sense of proportion, too." From the animation, Chesney then constructed a three-foot mock-up of the trimaran to further work out difficult design issues.

With plans and construction for the trimarans initiated, it was possible to focus on the other key defining element of the film—the atoll. Gassner knew that designing and building a full-scale set on water was an enormous undertaking—one, in fact, that had never before been approached on this scale. Drawings gave an idea of the scope of the project, but Gassner knew that building a set of this nature called for more information than two-dimensional illustrations could provide. He decided that a floating model was a better way to conceptualize what the set would be like full-scale. "The decision to build the atoll was a big decision," he noted. "A very big decision. So we had John Dexter, who is a set designer,

build an eleven-foot model to give people an idea of what we were getting into. We needed to see how the atoll looked in the water, how big it was, and understand the logic that went into designing the piece, as well as how it would facilitate the action in the script. It was also a better way to estimate the cost, and it gave us an idea of some of the problems we would be facing. The atoll was a working sculpture. It was something I'd never done before—it was something *nobody* had ever done before. And we had one other important consideration: time. We knew that if we wanted to shoot by a certain date, plans for the atoll needed to begin immediately."

They did. Once the atoll model was constructed, it was sent to a ship-model testing facility in San Diego. The designers knew it was essential to make the atoll as structurally sound as possible; they also knew that rigorous testing would help troubleshoot potential problems. They were facing challenges that could only be imagined at this point. The atoll was completely unique; there were no guidelines for designing and constructing something of this nature. Furthermore, the atoll was not going to be an ordinary movie set. It had to be built to survive, quite literally, in the open sea. Dennis Gassner, David Klassen, Steve Burg, and Peter Chesney began working on designs based on the model, and came up with plans for what was to become the largest floating articulated structure in the world. The completed atoll set would eventually reach a 365-foot diameter, and measure a quarter mile in circumference.

Although a circular formation had always been indicated, the designers wanted to avoid anything too obviously symmetrical. It was determined that separate sections of varying sizes and shapes, linked together, would best represent the different parts of the floating city. This offered the best structural solution, while making perfect sense storywise. For example, they knew that the Mariner's trimaran needed to sail into the atoll through large gates, and that the Mariner then needed to conduct business at some sort of trading post. They also recognized that the city would have an infrastructure with leadership and laws that had been established over generations of living adrift at sea. These kinds of considerations were factored into the design. Earlier illustrations had reflected this as well, and an even larger, more elaborate city had been considered—but as soon as the logistics of building the full-scale set became clear, ideas were pared down to a more manageable size. It was determined that nine separate, multilevel sets joined together to form a larger unit would serve as home to the Atollers, and would include entry gates, a fishery, an assay office, a factory, a meeting hall and tavern, a combination desalination plant and Gregor's Tower, the Organo Barge, and an armory.

As plans for the atoll progressed, it became immediately apparent that a major challenge had yet to be considered—how were they going to keep the floating city afloat? "Part and parcel to discovering how we were actually going to make the atoll," recalled Gassner, "was realizing that we also needed a way to make it float. I'll always remember the day I called Peter Chesney, who was hard at work figuring out how to make the trimaran transform. The trimaran was a very, *very* big design challenge. I said to him, 'There's just one other little problem. How are we going to make the atoll float?' He thought a moment and said, 'I think it's going to take a long time to figure that out.' So Peter went to work. Besides being an effects person with a physics background, he's also a sailor. He's been sailing all his life, he knows boats, and he's an experienced diver. He knows everything about the water. We went through months of discussions and planning, but finally

Peter figured out a way to make it float. He had the incredible talent to come up with a simple solution—although arriving at it was anything *but* simple." Chesney's simple solution ended up being a series of large, very stable steel barges made of colvert tubes and ten-inch I-beams upon which could be built a foundation for the set. This created a grid flotation system that followed the contours of the circular atoll design. However, a significant problem remained. The construction of such devices was beyond the technical skill of even the most experienced movie production crews. Gassner had earlier approached construction coordinator John Villarino with the dilemma. "John and his crew had done *Jurassic Park*, and he's a wonderful coordinator, one of the best in the business. John looked at plans for the atoll and said, 'You give me a stage floor, something solid to build on, and I'll build on top of it. Anything below that is not my department.' I knew he was right, of course. The difficulty was finding someone who could and would do the job."

The *Waterworld* design team immediately began searching for an answer to the problem and found one in a surprising place. Early on, Gassner had contacted a couple of local boat dealers and asked them to obtain as many boats as possible for the film. The thinking was that boats in various sizes from around the islands would help create the set, and Gassner knew he needed at least a hundred. While looking around boat warehouses and shipyards for this purpose, the boat dealers had noticed a company in Honolulu called Navitech that had designed an unusual, eye-catching boat. A contact was made and it was discovered that Navitech was a subsidiary of Lockheed, the engineering company known for designing the fastest jet airplane in the world—the SR-71. Gassner and Chesney approached Lockheed with the unusual request to build the foundation for a floating, futuristic city. Lockheed was understandably surprised, but found the new engineering challenge very appealing. After much discussion and planning, they agreed to design a flotation foundation for the atoll and Navitech agreed to build it.

* * *

By January 1994, Kevin Reynolds had completed principal photography on the physically challenging *Rapa Nui* and returned to Los Angeles to focus his attention on *Waterworld*. That same month, Dennis Gassner and the art department moved some of their preproduction operations to the Port of Kawaihae, where the production company had begun the process of transforming an isolated marina and abandoned sugar shack into a viable movie studio. Renamed King Kona Productions, the new studio began in earnest the Herculean efforts necessary to begin filming *Waterworld* by late spring. Location manager Ginger Peterson, who had started in October, dealt with basic production essentials such as obtaining permits; renting trailers for offices, dressing rooms, and studios; arranging housing; ordering power lines and telephone equipment; and dealing with fences, air conditioning, and transportation needs. The countless conveniences taken for granted under normal Hollywood circumstances had to be carefully procured for the location shoot.

Construction of the trimarans had begun at Jeanneau around the first of September. By February 10, they were ready to be shipped, in sections, to the *Waterworld* set in Hawaii. Under ordinary conditions, boats of this size would have been transported on the deck of a freighter—a job that would have taken a month to accomplish. In the case of the two, sixty-by-forty-five-foot custom-made trimarans, however, there wasn't a month to spare. The production schedule simply could not accommodate such a luxury. It was determined that if they were shipped in pieces via truck from France to Luxembourg, the boats could be tightly stowed into the body of a 747 air freighter and flown to Kona from the airport there. Upon their arrival in Hawaii, the trimarans emerged from the nose of the jet and were lifted onto a specially made conveyor and hydraulic-lift rig. They were then carefully loaded into trucks that took them back to the *Waterworld* sugar shack where they were assembled by Bruno Belmont and a fourteen-person crew that had flown over from France. A month later, the trimarans were in the water with Belmont and crew refining the intricate workings of the crafts, and training for their roles as invisible sailors.

Lockheed had begun engineering flotation for the atoll based on design parameters set by Chesney and the art department. Set designers Richard Mays and Marco Rubeo were added to the staff and immediately began drafting blueprints for the intricate structure, while construction crews simultaneously began to build it. "The atoll was a living sculpture in a sense," said Gassner, "and a mad metamorphosis began to take place: design, engineering, and construction all happening at the same time. It

"Under ordinary conditions, boats of this size would have been transported on the deck of a freighter . . . [but] there wasn't a month to spare."

was so big, and we were so pressed for time, and it was all so new. The atoll was something that had never been done before, so nobody could say, 'You do it this way.' We had to figure everything out from scratch, every single detail. And there were a lot of details—we were swimming in them. It was beyond anybody's expectation."

Basic questions were raised and needed to be answered immediately and correctly. How would they move the atoll? How should they anchor it—and with what? What was the best way to connect the eight separate flotation barges that would create the foundation for the nine key sets? Where could camera equipment be set up? The critical issue of safety engulfed them at every turn. Another key factor was weight. "It became a weight management issue," explained Gassner, "a design and weight management issue. Every piece of steel that was on top of the barge flotation system had to be weighed before it could be added. Each individual unit had to float like a boat. We were basically designing boats with centers of gravity and safety factors. A major consideration was knowing that the atoll had to go from a harbor system to a deep water system. We did a wind analysis, which was added into the design parameters for Lockheed. The unit was designed to be towed in forty-five knot winds at a speed of one-and-a-half knots, to be safe. Forty-five knot winds are hurricane-force winds, so we knew it was something the atoll could take '"

By February, delivery of the customized steel flotation units designed by Lockheed and built by Navitech was ready to begin. Shipped on barges towed by tugboats, the flotation units were transported in a 200-mile, twenty-four-hour voyage from the Honolulu shipyard where they were constructed. Once they arrived at Kawaihae, however, another significant challenge lay ahead—getting them safely off the barges and into the harbor. When the first flotation unit arrived, there were no cranes available on the Big Island to lift the fragile, eighty-ton unit into the water. Peter Chesney devised a system of inch-thick twenty-five-ton steel spuds—long stakes frequently used in dredging—that hung off the side of the barge. The spuds served as rollers to ease the mammoth vessel into the water—a task that took a crew of stevedores a grueling thirty-six hours to accomplish. By the time the second flotation unit arrived, a new technique was ready to be pioneered. This time the flotation unit was flooded with desalted sea water to add enough weight to lower the barge itself. Extensions were added to the flotation unit's delicate steel I-beams for protection. The flotation was then wrestled into the harbor and the water was pumped out. By the time the third flotation unit was ready for delivery, two 200-ton cranes had been obtained, and were in position to assist in its removal from the barge. Although still an unwieldy, time- and labor-intensive process, the cranes served to simplify the myriad logistical problems somewhat. By March 15, 1994, all the flotation units had been delivered by Navitech. Placed end to end along the pier in Kawaihae Harbor, they formed a line over 1,000 feet long.

While John Villarino's construction crews labored at full force, the script was refined more completely. The story line was trimmed and simplified; action elements were heightened. Battle sequences between the Mariner and the Smokers were detailed more clearly. The Deacon's character, which had always had religious undertones, became more of a cultlike figure, and his decidedly nasty sense of humor was tuned up to an even nastier pitch. The Deacon's penchant for children as servants and potential disciples—an element that Peter Rader had touched on in earlier drafts— was developed even further. Costner, Reynolds, and Gordon continued to

The design of Enola's tattoo evolved along with the story. The single circle brushed with Chinese characters was based on an image created by Kevin Reynolds. Once the tattoo's design was finalized, makeup artist Fred Blau, Jr., transformed it into stencils that were applied to Tina Majorino's back.

work with writer David Twohy in the area of character enrichment for the enigmatic Mariner, as well as at developing more fully the Mariner's relationship with the child, Enola. The story line had evolved from a fanciful, no-holds-barred epic to a gritty, fairly straightforward action-adventure—while still retaining the environmental overtones that were important to all concerned. The climactic third act of the movie—the lengthy, thrill-a-minute action sequence that would bring the Mariner, Helen, and Enola to the 'Deez, for the final confrontation with the Deacon and the Smokers—remained elusive, however, and Twohy and the filmmakers continued their efforts to satisfactorily chisel it out.

Although the trimaran and atoll had been the most immediate concerns the art department and construction crews faced, other areas of *Waterworld* also demanded attention. The darker realm of the Deacon and his ruthless band of Smokers needed to be established and brought to life, as well. The Smokers' grimy reality of conspicuous consumption and ultimate waste created a formidable contrast to the Atollers' more ecologically based philosophy. "The 'Deez is basically our bad guys' atoll," explained art director David Klassen. "They have taken possession of this immense 1,200-foot-long supertanker—which is about four football fields placed one end to the other. There are supposed to be up to 5,000 people living there, and they are in a pretty desperate state of poverty and chaos. It's not unlike World War II where a lot of hopeless people who had no leadership turned to Hitler. In Waterworld, they turn to the Deacon. The Smokers have found a way to refine oil and use it to power their armada, which includes jetskis, WaveRunners, and various other barges and boats. They've also found a way to manufacture all their own bullets, which they do by tearing apart their own ship for the metal to melt and mold. It's interesting from a cinematic standpoint, because where do you get a 1,200-foot-long supertanker? Do you buy one? We went through that scenario and it would have been tremendously expensive. It would also have been logistically very tough for the shooting company because tankers stand ninety feet out of the water when they're empty, and we would have had to crane the company and equipment up and down that tremendous distance—which would have taken an incredible amount of work and time. It was also impossible from an ecological point of view; there could have been as much as 100,000 gallons of sludge left over in the pipes. You can't put people into that kind of environment, and you can't wash it out."

It was decided instead to construct a 550-foot top deck for the 'Deez using forced perspective to make it appear to be the requisite 1,000 feet in length. The filmmakers found a warehouse owned by Pacific Tube Company in the City of Commerce, near Los Angeles, which had recently served as a location for the movie *Patriot Games*. The 1,000-foot-long warehouse was perfect for interior shots and, best of all, it boasted an adjacent 2,000-foot-field where the top deck of the tanker could be built. Because the script called for the Deacon's scout plane to land on the tanker's runway, it was essential to provide an appropriate landing space. The Los Angeles construction crew was scheduled to begin work sometime in July, with computer-generated water to be added later on in postproduction under the supervision of visual effects coordinator Micheal McAlister. Much of the climactic third act battle sequence would be shot at this location, after the cast and crew had completed filming in Hawaii and returned to the mainland.

Meanwhile, the workload in Hawaii during the months of April and May was intensive. Crews of as many as 500 workers labored in the tropical heat on the massive atoll set, as well as on the innumerable boats, sets, props, and costumes that made up the rest of the waterborne civilization. Special effects supervisor Marty Bresin signed on to begin coordinating the heavy-duty effects that would be used throughout the complex shoot, which had been rescheduled to begin in late June. The production itself had become an epic; *Waterworld* had reached a size and scope beyond anyone's initial expectations. The challenge of facing the ocean had been bravely met, but it was taking its toll. Concerns about cost and the rapidly approaching shooting schedule weighed heavily on the filmmakers as they continued their all-out efforts to realize their unprecedented cinematic vision.

Capturing that vision on screen would require the skills of an experienced cinematographer, and Dean Semler joined the first-rate production team as director of photography. Semler's efforts on *Dances with Wolves* had earned him an Academy Award for cinematography, and he was well versed in the futuristic action-adventure genre, having performed similar duties for *Mad Max* in 1979 and *Mad Max 2: The Road Warrior* in 1981. The veteran DP had also served on *Dead Calm*, a 1989 Australian thriller set aboard a yacht, as well as on *Cocktail, Young Guns, Young Guns II, City Slickers, The Last Action Hero, The Three Musketeers*, and *The Cowboy Way. Waterworld* would mark his reassociation with Kevin Costner and the Gordons, while offering the unparalleled challenge of filming a world set completely on water.

Costume designer for *Waterworld* would be John Bloomfield, who had worked most recently with Kevin Reynolds on *Rapa Nui*, as well as serving earlier on *Robin Hood: Prince of Thieves*. Bloomfield was experienced in creating visually rich apparel for such period films as *A Man for All Seasons* and *Christopher Columbus*, as well as for the distinctive PBS series, *The Six Wives of Henry the Eighth. Waterworld* offered him the opportunity to project a vision of an era yet to come.

Gathering the actors who would breathe life into *Waterworld*'s ensemble of characters was another essential part of preproduction. The process had begun, of course, when Kevin Costner signed on to play the Mariner. Apart from the actor's personal commitment to the role from the inception of the project, he was the perfect epic hero—talented, athletic, and one of the biggest box office stars in the world.

Casting director David Rubin and associates led the search to fill *Waterworld's* remaining roles. It was determined that Jeanne Tripplehorn would play the part of Helen. The actress had gained some prominence in the role of Tom Cruise's multifaceted wife in *The Firm*, and had earlier created a memorable screen presence as Michael Douglas's girlfriend in *Basic Instinct*. Tripplehorn possessed the combination of tenderness and tenacity that seemed to define the character of Helen.

Another key role was Enola, the little girl who would lead them all to the film's legendary Dryland. The filmmakers took their time in casting such a pivotal role. They knew that the young actress chosen for the part would be put to a substantial test both physically and artistically. While considering the part of Enola, they happened to see the film *When a Man Loves a Woman*, starring Meg Ryan and Andy Garcia as a married couple struggling with the problem of alcoholism. Tina Majorino played their daughter, and once the filmmakers saw her singular performance, there was no doubt as to who would make a perfect Enola. Majorino was immediately offered the part.

The pivotal role of Gregor, the inventor/wizard of the atoll who serves as a friend to Helen and an ally to the Mariner, would go to Michael Jeter. Jeter's career had begun with *Hair* and included *Tango and Cash*, *The Fisher King*, and *Sister Act II*, along with one of television's most popular shows, *Evening Shade*. A veteran of the stage as well, Jeter was the ideal choice for the befuddled genius. Jeter was drawn to the project because of the unique decision to film on water and by the challenge of playing a character so much older than himself.

The search for the right actor to play the part of the Mariner's archenemy, the Deacon, remained somewhat elusive, however, and the filmmakers continued to seek out the person who could convey the combination of humor and evil so integral to the story.

By June the trimarans had long been assembled, but crews continued the involved process of rigging and finessing that would make them camera-ready by the end of the month. Workers labored day and night to complete the atoll in time for the beginning of principal photography. As work on the impressive structure neared completion, several local Hawaiians approached the production company about a matter of some significance; to ensure a safe and successful venture, a blessing for the atoll was advised. A similar ceremony had taken place at the beginning of construction. The gesture of good luck and goodwill made sense to the *Waterworld* production company, and it was decided to invite the local shaman, or kahuna, to conduct a special ceremony of blessing. The entire production company, cast, and crew were joined by local dignitaries and business people for the blessing and exchange of good intentions.

Finally, after a year and a half of intensive, groundbreaking preparation, principal photography for *Waterworld* commenced on Monday, June 27, 1994. The cast and crew were assembled on the atoll where a shot of the gates opening and the Mariner sailing through had been set up and was ready to go. The excitement was palpable. It had been an enormous undertaking and required the commitment of hundreds of dedicated people to make this day possible.

"Originally they had wanted to cast someone around the age of Sir Alec Guinness," Jeter said, "but they realized that someone that age would not be able to sustain the physical load of the part. They decided to cast **GREGOR** younger so that the actor would be able to keep up with the work. Of course, that meant changing the character a bit, but I really think of Gregor as ageless. I was also intrigued by the milieu of the picture; the idea that the world as we know it is not here anymore, just the floating remnants—and that those who are left have to piece it all together."

"**ENOLA** is a very strong character," observed Majorino. "She's got a lot of courage and she knows what she wants. She helps other people have courage, too. She's very special to Helen because she's Helen's adopted child. But to other people, like the Atollers, she's very different and unusual—some people think she's trouble. It's different with Enola and Gregor. They have a very, *very* tight connection. He's sort of like a grandpa to her. They're both the same kind of people—different, but smart."

"We knew there would be difficulties shooting on water," stated Costner, "but there are also opportunities created inside any difficulty. What becomes possible or impossible on land? There are limitations no matter where you shoot. We knew it would be hard dealing with the ocean, but we decided to meet the challenge."

2. LIFE ON AN ENDLESS SEA

Water, water, every where,
And all the boards did shrink;
Water, water, every where,
Nor any drop to drink.
Samuel Taylor Coleridge

Opening images don't get any more vivid than this one: a lone sailor on a lonely sea stands aboard the worn deck of his vessel and urinates into a Pyrex beaker. He pours the liquid into an elaborate purifying system and then swallows the recycled swill in a gulp. It is our first and most indelible impression of the Mariner—a man so completely self-sufficient that he has managed to transform even the most basic of elements into a resource for survival. It is an eloquent introduction to Waterworld.

The Mariner's remarkable vessel is revealed in an expansive scan. Beyond the urine purifier, it seems he has a knack for adapting the innumerable objects he scavenges from the ocean floor. It also becomes clear that the Mariner is in possession of mutated webbed feet, a useful adaptation in this watery world—but one that will cause him considerable discomfort socially. The Mariner dives into the water and, upon emerging from an unusually lengthy underwater stay, has an encounter with a solitary drifter. The Mariner's salvage bag floats in the background. The two men establish a mutually comprehensible language—a variety of languages are dabbled with throughout the film—and the Mariner suggests a trade. The drifter declines, having just visited an atoll some eight days east. With this scene, we begin to understand some of the unwritten laws of Waterworld and get an initial glimpse into the lives

The crew assembles the trimaran directly on the water.

A crane unloads the trimaran onto the dock.

its people must lead. Their brief meeting is rudely interrupted by the arrival of a band of Smokers on jetskis. We see the Mariner move into action as he trips the various switches that cause the trimaran to transform from a lumbering trawler into a heroic escape boat. Behind the mask of a tinker, we discover Ulysses.

In its way, the Mariner's trimaran is as much a featured performer as the actors. Dennis Gassner made sure it was equipped to reflect the nobility of the Mariner's heroism, while establishing his down-and-dirty ingenuity. "When I first saw the original Jeanneau racing trimaran I knew it was the perfect boat," recalled Gassner. "I said to Kevin Costner, 'This is wonderful, but I think we need to do something that's unique. You're our superhero and we want you to have toys to facilitate that.' I figured that one man sitting in a boat all day long would have a lot of time on his hands. Beyond that, there must have been generations and generations of families that lived on the boat before him. I figured they were probably creative people who would have found inventive ways to facilitate their daily needs.

"I loved the Japanese 'Transformers' that were out a few years ago—those toys that could change from one kind of machine to another. I had little collections of them and have always been fascinated with seeing things that transform and become something else. I knew we needed to modify the trimaran in the same way. We decided the Mariner was basically a scavenger—he dealt with taking things off the bottom and reworking them or selling them. But how did he do that? We had to find a way to demonstrate his inventiveness. If the trimaran looked like a sleek sailing boat the whole time, that wouldn't have sold the idea. That's why we came up with the trawling mode as the answer. I turned to Peter Chesney and asked him, 'Can you do this physically?' And he said, 'Yes.'"

It had been decided that two trimarans would best accomplish the job—one to be used solely for sailing purposes, the other to serve both as the trawler and to perform the transformation sequence. For the trawling version, they came up with an eggbeater-style windmill rotor blade that would serve as a dredge under peaceful circumstances, while transforming into a sturdy mast when a quick getaway was indicated. They figured that the Mariner would have "kludged" together a windmill rotor that went through a gearbox to run a propeller, thus making it possible for him to trawl on the bottom of the ocean with some kind of strength—kludged being Waterworld lingo for reworking found objects into something new and useful. "The idea that drove the design work was that there was no stored energy in Waterworld," explained Chesney. "They didn't have big batteries, they didn't have fuel for engines, and there were no vacuum-packed flywheels—it was all wind energy. So we gave the Mariner geared-down power through the windmill; if he were to go slow and drag hard, he could really scoop stuff up from the bottom. The windmill rotor also gave him the power for the big winch in the back, as well as the power to run the little bit of electricity he did have. Also, the Mariner has had a lifetime to build and gadgetize, and with his ability to dive, he would have been able to find parts out of old machinery. For instance, the little gearbox in the back was an old Ford truck transmission. We actually drove the little electric motor and made the shift linkage work. The helm of the trimaran was designed to be both a steering and a crank helm, which also reflected the Mariner's inventiveness. Besides that, a standing position where he could spring into action was much more heroic than having him stuck at an ordinary wheel."

In the movie, the trimaran transforms from trawling to sailing mode when the Mariner moves quickly from stanchion to stanchion, flipping the switches that cause a remarkable chain of events. First, the eggbeater blades of the windmill fold into the mast, then the mast lengthens to twice its height and the boom lifts from out of the deck with the sails unfurling quickly into position. It is an effect that appears to take about ten seconds, but one that, in reality, required considerably more time, effort, and planning—along with six people coordinating the choreography. Counterweight bags were placed up on the mast and then lowered to start the transformation process. Then the twenty-five-foot eggbeater-shaped rotor—which had been spinning at approximately fifteen revolutions per minute—stopped and collapsed. The delicate rotor blades were also expected to hold their shape at speed without bowing out too much, a consideration that caused the designers some concern. Likewise, because the rotor was structurally very thin, the designers were aware that a rotational twist might unceremoniously rip

Cranes lifted the flotation units, which would buoy the atoll, into the water.

the ends off the blades. A composite engineer was hired to help determine a material that would provide both strength and flexibility. The solution was the same heat-cured high-grade epoxy fiberglass used in making top-quality hockey sticks. The fiberglass provided the lightness, strength, and flexibility necessary to endure the rigorous transformation process.

The eggbeater rotor assembly was driven by two hydraulic motors placed at the top and bottom. "The hardest part was keeping the hydraulics synchronized," said Chesney. "The wind was supposed to be causing them to move, but if the wind blew too hard they were difficult to control. There was so much momentum built up in the twenty-foot radius of the blades, that just starting them up and stopping them required the help of a computer. We actually used motion control hardware just to keep them synchronized."

The atoll attached to the shore in Kawaihae Harbor.

After the windmill folded, a cable attached to a hydraulic motor and drum pulled the telescoping mast up thirty feet, lengthening it to an impressive height of eighty-five feet. As the mast went up, the main halyard—the line that hoisted the sail—pulled out of the deck and lifted the boom from a special spring-loaded hatch that had been built into the deck. The boom sprang up on an eccentric cam arm from its customized twelve-foot hatch and extended to an amazing thirty feet in length. To accomplish this, the boom was constructed as a four-piece compound extension. It was made out of hand-bent aluminum for two compelling reasons: to match the appearance of the sailing trimaran's boom and to be structurally sound enough to carry a lightweight sail for a short time. The sail was tucked and folded beneath the boom and was pulled up a track as the mast went up. The sail was connected at the tip of the boom, following the same design as competition sailboats.

Under ordinary racing conditions, the trimarans would have been made entirely out of pure carbon fiber—the mast, the pontoons, and the

boom—using a high-tech composite construction. Such boats would have been prohibitively expensive and besides that, as competitive racers they far exceeded the design criteria of the film. The modified *Waterworld* trimarans, however, were made of a fiberglass and carbon-fiber blend with aluminum masts. The sails were fashioned out of Spectra, a high-strength material made of mono-linked polyethylene for maximum durability. The taut netting that linked the three separate hulls of the trimaran—and formed a working surface for cast and crew—was also made of Spectra. "Spectra is an incredibly strong material," said Chesney. "For instance, a piece of Spectra the size of a shoelace can hold as much as 6,000 pounds, compared to nylon, which could only support about 2,000 pounds. And Spectra doesn't stretch. That was important because the camera department needed a surface that was very firm and not at all trampolinelike. We also made sure to build in enough places for camera bridges to facilitate photography."

For director of photography Dean Semler, the trimaran offered more than enough potential camera setups. "We had platforms to cover that trimaran from one end to the other," he said. "We could literally put the camera anywhere on the trimaran and move it any place we wanted. The platforms were somewhat time-consuming to install, but they gave us all kinds of shooting options. We had platforms right on the front of the bow, we had them across the sides—we even had cameras right up at the top of the mast. We had to come up with a lot of special rigs for this film because it was so unique; nobody had ever shot something like this on water before, and everything was new. I'd shot *Dead Calm* and the *Mad Max* pictures—in a way *Waterworld* was a combination of the two—but I had never done a major 'action at sea' picture before. There was *so* much dialogue at sea; thirty or forty pages of the screenplay took place on the trimaran. That became the major challenge. It was something like trying to make a movie on the catch net in a circus."

Aside from the modifications required for the transformation sequence, design crews also had to accommodate the requirement that the trimaran be steered by a remote crew rather than by Costner, thus offering the actor the freedom to perform without having to manage a sixty-foot racing sailboat at the same time. Two separate compartments were built below deck. The forward compartment housed the pilot and copilot, who steered the boat's independent hydraulic system using a small joystick similar to a radio-controlled airplane. The rear compartment accommodated the crew responsible for operating the sail rigging and winches.

Naval architect and boat builder Bruno Belmont had been involved in the building of the trimarans from the inception of the project. During the shoot he served as trimaran coordinator, alternately sailing the boats with trimaran skipper Gary Hoover and their crew. "These boats can go as fast as twenty miles an hour," noted Belmont, "so the crew down below had to be responsible for sailing the trimarans. We had five television screens rigged at various points to show us what was going on above—one was placed in the masthead shooting forward, two were off the back, and two faced forward off the bow. A video switcher below deck permitted us to view crucial areas on a fourteen-inch monitor, while maintaining visual contact on smaller black-and-white monitors. We also had a hatch, so if there was an electronic or video failure, we could always stand up, pop our heads out of the hatch, and see where we were going—at least any time it was noncritical. We had to build a lot of control into the boat remotely because these shots weren't going to compromise." It was also possible to override this system entirely and permit Costner to manage the vessel himself during a more relaxed mode of sailing.

The steering section of the trimaran was also equipped for navigational purposes, such as monitoring the marine radios and plotting compass headings. Communication was maintained with the film crew via radio. "We had an autopilot, which was a system on the tiller of the boat that set and maintained the correct direction," explained Belmont. "It also helped us turn if we needed it to. Additionally, the trimarans were equipped with a boat-positioning system that worked with a satellite. For example, by using a map of Kawaihae and knowing the position of the boat, we could

The Organo Barge alongside the atoll's outer wall.

Most detail work on the atoll's construction was left for the interior views.

track where we were going and where we wanted to go. That system could be connected to the autopilot so we could program the trimaran's direction. The sailing trimaran was equipped with the ability to access more specific navigational information—the wind strength, the speed of the boat, the depth under the boat, and all the things that allowed us to be safe."

A typical sailing racer of this kind would ordinarily weigh about five and a half tons. Because of the additional equipment needed for their unique operational requirements, however, the *Waterworld* trimarans weighed in at approximately eight tons. As with the construction of the atoll, weight became an important safety consideration. "If the trimarans were to get too low in the water, with all the power the sail had," said Chesney, "the front end could have started pushing in, making the whole boat

capable of pitch-pulling. So trim and ballast became very important. We had to find ways to cut back on weight and, unfortunately, air-conditioning for the crew below deck was one of them. We had an electric fan and ventilation, but no air conditioner. Weight was very critical on that boat, and if it had gotten too low on the waterline it wouldn't have sailed."

An interior set of the trimaran was constructed in the sugar shack and dressed by set decorator Nancy Haigh and crew. Haigh worked closely with Dennis Gassner in determining the elements that would garnish the intricate sets throughout the film. They had first paired up on *Field of Dreams* and then again on *Bugsy* in 1991, for which they won an Academy Award. Haigh had most recently served as set decorator for *Forrest Gump*. She took a week off after completing her work on *Gump* in January, and headed straight for Hawaii. "In dressing the Mariner's cabin the crucial question was, 'What does this guy do all day?'" she observed. "The answer was, 'He dives.'"

"We did a lot of research on the *Titanic* and other diving expeditions of sunken ships and learned that when salvaged items surface, their condition is so bad they're almost unrecognizable. We had to come up with scavenged items for the Mariner, but we had to make sure that they were still recognizable. We needed items from all walks of life, especially tools—gardening tools, screwdrivers, pliers, and so on. Surprisingly, old items were hard to obtain. Actually, it was very easy to *find* old tools, they were just too expensive to buy because tool collecting in America is a big pastime and they have become collectors' items. So we bought new tools and the paint department aged them. They devised a way to barnacle and crust up and colorize these items, while maintaining the integrity of the shape. If we had *really* made them look like what comes up from the bottom of the sea, they would have been too disfigured to recognize. So the variety of tools we used—and shoes and ski poles and hats and helmets and buckets—all still looked like what they really were, just very crusted. We also made a worktable for the Mariner with the idea that he slowly cleans these things up and that they're the stash he trades when he reaches

The desalination tanks under construction and still connected to shore.

A sketch for the Organo Barge, showing some of the early Oriental influences on the set design.

an atoll. Kevin Costner requested certain things. He wanted rearview mirrors to trade and some hubcaps to carve weapons out of, so we made sure he had those items. We set this assortment of salvaged junk all around the worktable area to show how he spends some of his time. Further back in the cabin are things he hasn't even gotten around to yet."

* * *

In a vivid and daring escape sequence, the Mariner expertly snags his salvage bag and sails away from the Smokers in triumph. The next image of the trimaran reveals it drifting in the trawling mode under much calmer circumstances. The atoll rises alone in the distance. As the Mariner approaches, the relationship between the trimaran and the floating colony becomes abundantly clear for the first time. It is a magnificent impression; a tremendous cityscape on water that defies all previous expectations of what might have sprung from the human spirit.

The atoll also represented a tremendous spirit of the filmmakers, who designed and built it against all possible odds. "I had a rendering on my desk of the original concept for the atoll," noted Charles Gordon. "It was eight boats tied together in a circle. I used to look at it every now and then and marvel at how simply it all started. But once Dennis Gassner designed the atoll, and we realized what we wanted to achieve on film, we just went with it. We never cared for the idea of using miniatures; it simply wouldn't have given us what we wanted—which was to be able to shoot a full-scale action-adventure movie on a full-size set. Once we made the commitment to creating the atoll as a full-size set, we never looked back. We wanted it so badly, especially because it seemed so right for the picture we were trying to make. It was scary, but it was also very exciting to be doing something of that scale."

And the scale was impressive. The eight separate flotation units that had been designed by Lockheed started weighing in at sixty-five tons—prior to the addition of any of the towers, catwalks, boats, and other structures that made up the sets. "As the flotation barges were delivered they were placed in a line all along the dock," explained David Klassen. "We did not put them all together until the set on each unit was completed enough to where they could be joined. We had to deal with problems and make little adjustments along the way to make certain everything would work. We started off with our concept and design, but we knew things would change because we were dealing with water—and they did. We had to make critical calls and decisions on the spot because we didn't have time to sit there and wait around."

The weight factor was the biggest redesign consideration. "The weight factor was incredible," said Klassen. "Everything we put on each one of the flotation units had to be weighed, and in order to do that we had to have a good weight management system. Weight was crucial because we had to have twenty-seven inches of freeboard—that meant twenty-seven inches between the deck and the water level. If we had gone down below that, it wouldn't have had the stability it needed to withstand the forty-five-knot winds and three-foot seas we had factored into the design parameters. We had to be prepared for what might happen when we moved the atoll from the sheltered harbor area out to deep water. The weight factor came into play as we got closer to that twenty-seven-inch margin. We were nearly 400 tons too heavy, so we had to find ways to cut back. It was a big job to remove tonnage without removing detail. We had to make sure the production value was there, so we removed things that wouldn't be visible on film. The atoll was an extraordinarily difficult kind of set to build. Building it on land would have been an ambitious project, but to build it on water was a truly amazing feat."

It was determined that considerable ballast could be eliminated by removing portions of the decking that had been placed on the flotation barges as a stage floor. "By cutting down on the amount of decking we were able to eliminate a lot of weight," Klassen said. "We also removed some of the

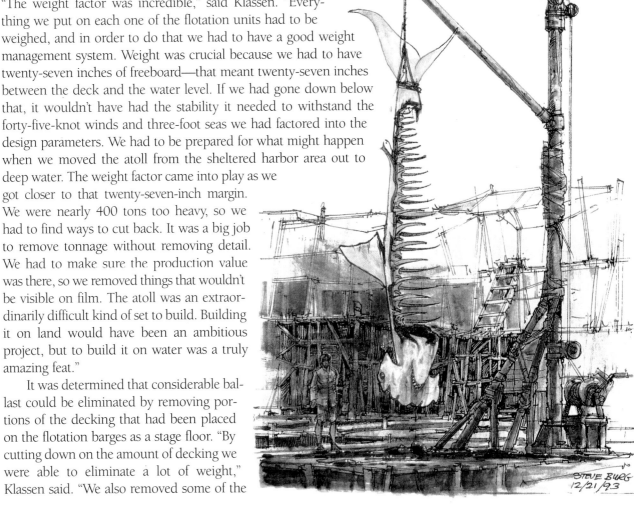

An enormous gutted shark hanging from a pulley device—designers thought through every aspect of how Atollers might actually live.

STEVE BURG
12/21/93

Cinematographer Dean Semler
on high in Gregor's loft.

KEVIN COSTNER'S HAWAII UH-OH

Over budget and out of time, the makers of *Waterworld* may be taking a historic bath

Sunset

▲ *Waterworld*'s big battle scene involved 125 extras and 50 stuntmen on Jet Skis.

◀ Kevin Reynolds (on the *Robin Hood* set) was director, but Kevin Costner, says a crew member, "ran the show."

➤ "If a film's in trouble," Costner (as Mariner) once said, "I can go in and fix it."

SPLASH

REX USA

BEN GLASS/UNIVERSAL

SOME 200 YEARS AGO, KING KAME-hameha I, ruler of the Big Island of Hawaii, built a temple on a bluff overlooking Kawaihae Harbor. The king dedicated the shrine to the war gods and offered up human sacrifices. Last May, one month before Kevin Costner's epic *Waterworld* began shoot-ing in the pristine waters outside the har-bor, 300 members of the cast and crew gathered on the pier and made their own attempt to appease the deities, enlisting a kahuna (high priest) to bless the site. "We wanted the ceremony," says Wayne Awai, 46, a local crew member, "because we thought it would be a good omen."

It wasn't. That same month, *Water-world*'s female lead, Jeanne Tripplehorn, and 12-year-old actress Tina Majorino were aboard a trimaran, a French-built sailboat, when suddenly the bowsprit snapped, plunging both actresses into the sea. Nearly a dozen rescue divers jumped in after them and quickly brought them back on board.

Nor was that the only close call. In De-cember, Costner, one of the movie's pro-ducers and its star, was strapped 40 feet in the air to the mast of a sailboat. Sud-denly, ferocious winds whipped up and

◄ "He cannot understand the permanence of what has happened," a psychologist says of Danny (skimming stones).

▲ "Every day, even when he was not here, we would talk to him as if he were," says Daniela (frolicking with Danny at home).

▲ "Anything you play," notes Kirchner (with Danny and his pals), he says, 'I win.' "

The Lion King and Power Ranger lore. He plays with the neighborhood kids, rides his training bike around the pond behind the apartment building, and within a week of the transfer he was calling the Kirchners Mom and Dad.

Kirchner has plenty of time to spend with his son: he has been unemployed since the restaurant he was managing closed last summer. The family is supported by Daniela, a beautician, while Otakar hopes for movie offers to defray his $400,000 in legal bills. He and Danny continue to bond over Nerf ball, Super Nintendo and other pursuits—such as the toy race track now set up on the floor in front of the TV. Sometimes their recreations take a darker turn: "He is always shooting me with something, and I have to die," Kirchner says with a smile.

Still bitter, he and his wife are not likely to grant visitation rights to Robert and Kim Warburton. Daniela, however, says she would welcome their son John: "He can come here and play—that's fine. But not the parents."

According to Karen Moriarty, a psychologist who makes daily visits to observe the Kirchners, the boy is adapting well to his new environs. Remarkably, Moriarty insists, Danny has never mentioned the Warburtons. "Can I lie to you and say it isn't so?" asks the psychologist. "Every day I'm keeping notes."

But Bennett Leventhal, an expert on childhood trauma who chairs the University of Chicago's child and adolescent psychiatry department, doubts that Danny is emotionally unscathed by his experience. "The kid is going to be scarred for life," he says bluntly. "Anybody who pretends this will all go away and he'll live happily ever after is wrong."

Perhaps. But on this May afternoon, Danny and Kirchner are engaged in the ultimate American father-son rite. The boy is on an imaginary pitcher's mound in the yard, rubber ball in hand, screwing up his face like a scowling big-leaguer, a Cubs hat turned backward on his head. Taking a sign from an invisible catcher, he fires an impressive heater at Kirchner that whizzes off course into the pond nearby. "Oh, no!" the boy moans.

"Don't worry," says his father, his 280-pound bulk hurtling toward the water's edge. "Daddy will get it. Daddy will get it."

■ RICHARD JEROME
■ BRYAN ALEXANDER *in Chicago, and bureau reports*

at the time was clinging, terrified, to Kim Warburton. He is distinctly ambivalent about Danny's apparent hysteria en route to the waiting van. "It was not like real crying with tears falling down," he says. "It was like cats meowing." But in the next breath, Kirchner, more pensive, makes an astonishing claim: "If I had known that after four years I would have to see my son cry, I would have never started this case."

In any event, he says Danny calmed down immediately while sitting on his mother's lap in the van. "I told him, I want to live with you, play with you, love you," recalls Kirchner. And when Kirchner made a hand puppet out of a plastic bag, he says he drew laughs from his son. As the van neared a McDonald's restaurant, Danny called out for Chicken McNuggets, and the three Kirchners passed through the golden arches like millions of other families.

That kind of mundane normality, of course, is their ultimate goal. Danny's bedroom is decorated with pictures of dalmatians and myriad images from

Costner was pelted by seawater, his body hammered against the mast. For 30 minutes, the crew stood by helplessly, knowing it was too dangerous to lower Costner to safety. "I nearly died," he told a friend later.

Mishaps often occur on a movie set, but there was hardly an uneventful day during the making of *Waterworld*. The thriller is set in the future, after a massive glacial meltdown has left most of the planet submerged. Costner stars as Mariner, a mutant creature with gills and fins, who tries to lead a group of survivors to dry land. The movie could yet turn out to be a spectacular hit: the *Jurassic Park* of 1995. Yet since the summer of 1993, when preproduction began, *Waterworld* has been, says production designer Dennis Gassner, "18 months of hell," owing to everything from bad weather to the complexities of pumping sewage from the dozens of floating toilets.

This is a movie that started big and kept getting bigger. Universal first estimated it would cost $65 million and take four months to shoot. Today, *Waterworld*'s budget has reportedly bloated to an unprecedented $175 million, some $55 million more than the cost of

BEN GLASS/UNIVERSAL

BEN GLASS/UNIVERSAL/SPLASH

◄ To get the weathered look of people at sea, all actors, including Jeanne Tripplehorn (left) and Tina Majorino, were given full body makeup.

➤ Costner often meditated outside his $1,800-a-night bungalow at the Mauna Lani Bay Hotel, which came with a private pool, butler and chef.

SPLASH

1994's *True Lies*, the previous most expensive movie of all time. *Waterworld* took eight months to make, and Costner is closeted now in the editing room, racing to meet the film's premiere date of July 28.

What went wrong? Eventually, just about everything. Scores of cast and crew members, including Costner, were afflicted with debilitating attacks of seasickness as they shot scenes on boats, barges and man-made islands. One major set sank under 180 feet of water, necessitating a costly salvage job. Costner's stuntman came up from a dive too fast one day and suffered a near-fatal case of the bends. Jellyfish stung everyone's legs and shoulders. And three weeks ago the movie's di-

rector, Kevin Reynolds, quit after battling with Costner and the studio over their visions of the film. "Costner wanted to do a heroic Errol Flynn-type movie," says Gassner, "but Reynolds wanted a less passionate character."

For its still boyishly handsome, 40-year-old star, the shoot was agonizing. Though he was earning $14 million and living in a $1,800-a-night oceanside bungalow, Costner looked, says one extra, "like he needed a hug." No wonder. After a string of hits, his recent movies *A Perfect World* and *The War* had bombed big-time. And though Costner took time off from *Waterworld* to promote *Wyatt Earp*, that turned out to be another flop. Meanwhile his personal relationships were collapsing.

Reynolds had been an old friend of Costner's, his handpicked director on 1991's *Robin Hood: Prince of Thieves*. And in October, Costner announced that he and his wife, Cindy, who have three children, were ending their 16-year marriage.

Though Costner is praised by crew members for being friendly and accessible, he couldn't avoid reminders of his personal troubles. Encountering an extra reading a tabloid that had Costner's marital problems splashed across its cover, he said politely but firmly, "I don't want to see that here again."

Waterworld wasn't always such a pit of money and misfortune. Written in the late '80s by a recent Harvard grad named Peter Rader, it was originally

◄ "I'd never been on a film before where no one ever said, 'You can't do that. It costs too much,' " says a crew member who worked on *Waterworld*'s set.

➤ "If you do things correctly, they have a way of working out," Costner (at a May 2 golf outing in L.A.) once said. "My karma has always been very good."

bought by tiny New World Pictures and budgeted at $3 million. Two years ago, when Universal took on the project, it was budgeted at almost $10 million more than the $56 million *Jurassic Park*. By the time production started, the tab had risen to nearly $100 million.

What made *Waterworld* so expensive, in the end, was the water. Almost every scene had to be shot on a floating set. Three hundred workers toiled for three months to build the movie's main stage, a 1,000-ton atoll constructed from wood, papier-mâché and steel. During production thousands of locals were hired as construction workers, extras and divers. The movie, says one crew member, was "like a blank check."

For six weeks, 425 extras and crew had to be ferried every day to the atoll floating 1,000 yards offshore. "Some days," says one stuntman, "by the time we got out to the water, we'd have to break for lunch without having gotten a single shot." Shooting stopped for clouds, strong wind or when humpback whales came within camera range. Even on calm days ocean swells kept pulling the camera boats apart, meaning that the same scene would have to be shot four or five times to make sure the filming angles would match in the editing room. One 10-minute action scene, scheduled to take a week, ate up an entire month.

Waterworld is going to have to be a swimaway success to recoup its costs.

In order for the studio to break even, the movie will have to sell $265 million worldwide in tickets, thus rivaling the take of *The Silence of the Lambs*. Christopher Borde of Paul Kagan Associates, media analysts, sketches one scenario in which Waterworld earns $125 million in U.S. ticket sales, but makes up the difference in TV and video rights, overseas sales and merchandising tie-ins. Borde thinks it will be difficult, but Costner has made people eat their predictions before. Hollywood insiders thought he was crazy when he held up *The Bodyguard* for a year while he waited for Whitney Houston, who had never acted before, to star with him. *Bodyguard* went on to earn $370 million in worldwide box-office receipts. He was

also ridiculed for making his directing debut with *Dances with Wolves,* a 3-hour epic complete with subtitles. *Wolves* made $365 million worldwide and won Costner an Oscar as Best Director.

A recent screening of an unfinished cut of *Waterworld,* held in Sacramento, earned mixed reviews. "The sailing scenes and scenery were quite terrific," one viewer told the *Los Angeles Times,* but another griped, "The sharks looked fake." Coincidentally or not, a crew is now shooting additional shark footage. Make that $175 million—and counting.

■ SHELLEY LEVITT
■ LORENZO BENET *in Hawaii and* KRISTINA JOHNSON, TOM CUNNEFF *and* DANELLE MORTON *in Los Angeles*

LIFE WITHOUT JACKIE

In the year since Jacqueline Kennedy Onassis's death, her children have tried to fill the void left by her passing

PETE SOUZA

▲ **Jackie's simple gray tombstone lies next to her husband's at Arlington National Cemetery.**

▼ **John and Caroline shared a light moment at the May 8 Profile in Courage awards.**

PAULA A. SCULLY/GAMMA LIAISON

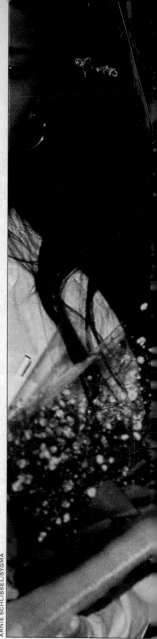

ARNIE SCHLISSEL/SYGMA

▲ **In March, Caroline spoke at a Manhattan ceremony in which the Midtown High School for International Careers renamed itself for Jacqueline Kennedy Onassis—a change students proposed shortly after Jackie's death.**

THE OVERCAST SKY WAS TYPICAL of Boston's late-arriving spring, and inside the Kennedy Library the tableau for the sixth presentation of the John F. Kennedy Profile in Courage Award seemed as it always had. On the dais sat Sen. Edward Kennedy, 63, and JFK's children, John F. Kennedy Jr., 34, and Caroline Kennedy Schlossberg, 37. The scene lacked just one familiar person: Jackie.

It has now been a year since Jacqueline Bouvier Kennedy Onassis died, at 64, of cancer in her New York City apartment. And the May 8 ceremony, imbued with memories of her first husband and the spirit of Camelot, brought her absence sharply to mind. Her son rose to speak, citing the past five recipients of an award that, he said, "reminds all citizens that politics remains an honorable profession." When Caroline presented former Oklahoma Rep. Mike Synar with the award—a sterling Tiffany lantern designed by her artist husband, Edwin, 49—she beckoned with Jackie-ish savvy for John to join her. At that moment it seemed another torch boats, cut down the size of the towers, and reduced the height of the walls, while still retaining the detail that was so essential to the design. Although they were coated to look like plastic, the walls were made of steel. We could only get certain types of steel on the island in the amount of time we had, so some of the steel weighed more than it was supposed to. When that happened, we had to cut in other areas."

Despite the removal of some of the decking to accommodate troublesome weight considerations, it remained an integral part of the atoll set. One acre of steel decking covered the eight flotation units to provide the surface that John Villarino and his crew required as a foundation for the set. "The decking provided the construction department with a continuous foundation," explained Peter Chesney, "but after they built the sets, crews put on swim fins and masks and cut out excess flooring that wouldn't be walked on." The decking was constructed with steel sub-beams for support and covered with a sturdy metal screening, which was coated to look like sea-weathered plastic. Architectural engineers were brought in to verify the structural safety. "The problem with this kind of metal screening was that it is not ordinarily used as a deck surface," Chesney continued. "The engineers were really in a quandary because they couldn't find it on any of their tables, and they weren't sure what to do. So we placed four guys as closely together as possible, and had them jump up and down and prove that it was plenty strong. It really held up. The steel deflected, but the more it bent, the stronger it got. We knew that if the deck ever overloaded, we didn't have to worry because it would just dish out a bit."

The steel mesh decking served a second extremely important function: if the atoll were to be exposed to big waves, the water would simply fall through the deck and not build up a water-plane surface on top. As little as two inches of water spilling across the deck would have represented enough weight to force the edges of the atoll under, thus creating the possibility of capsizing. The open weave of decking permitted the water to drain safely through while eliminating weight concerns.

* * *

As the Mariner sails his trimaran warily through the gates of the atoll, the city and its inhabitants are clearly revealed for the first time. The austere Atollers resemble Puritans in dress and manner, and though they admit the Mariner through their gates to trade, they offer him little kindness. "We wanted the people of the atoll to be from a repressed society," noted Dennis Gassner. "It was an important way to facilitate the action of the story, but it also helped create the mood. If the Mariner had come into a beautiful land like Oz, for example, he wouldn't have been accepted—he was far too

rough and ragged for that fantasy world. But in Waterworld, he is part of an acceptable norm. When I came onto the project I wanted to create a world that was totally unique, one that nobody had ever seen before. I wanted for it to be familiar and yet, somehow, unfamiliar. I think it started out as a very fascinating world, with people finding wonderful ways to adapt to their environment. After all, it is human nature to create something beautiful; we don't, by nature, create something that is ugly. I decided that if it were my world, I would create something that was functional while making it as interesting looking as possible. But then, because of time and evolution—and generations and generations of being on the water—things changed. Being on the water for any length of time is hard on the body; the constant physical movement is very draining. So we then had to figure out how such a society would evolve into the starchiness of Waterworld."

Gassner realized that hardship and deprivation would create a society held together by the most rigid of social mores. Surviving in a brutal world and facing the constant threat of attack by Smokers has left them wary of newcomers. The Atollers admit the Mariner through their gates as if it were a well-guarded medieval fortress. With that in mind, the designers were determined to create as primitive a look for this section as possible. "The Atollers have figured out a way to manufacture everything out of the plastics they have salvaged by using molds," explained David Klassen. "The technology of mold-making goes back to the fourteenth century and through the medieval period. We knew that the Atollers would have to figure out a way to make their tools, weapons, and structures *without* using some of the things we have available today—like computers and lasers—and would have to rely on pretty basic methods. In other words, they would have to reinvent the wheel. The design of the gates reflected this thinking."

The gates to the atoll were constructed on flotation number one, or F-1 —the letter "F" standing for flotation. The heaviest of all the flotations at 131 tons, F-1 was equipped with enormous bifolding doors and giant gears that actually turned. Two counterbalance weights were installed for each door—as one weight went down, the doors would open. To close them, the other weight would go back up. Hydraulic motors were installed to rotate the three-foot-thick frame of the outer gate, while an electric motor drove the sprocket that turned the one-and-a-half-foot inner gate. Each gate measured twenty-five feet in height and twelve feet in width; the unit folded to create a fifty-five-foot path—just wide enough to admit the forty-five-foot trimaran. Because the two sides of the gates had to match up precisely, the flotation was built as a single unit with I-beams joining the two sides five feet underwater, thus allowing the trimaran to sail over the connection. F-1 was the most delicate and problematic of all the flotation barges because of the working gates and towers attached to either side. The logistical height measured fifty-eight feet at the highest point, and additional flotation tubes were added to keep it safely balanced.

Walkways and camera platforms were factored into the multilevel design of the gates, as they were throughout the atoll. "The upper catwalks had the loading capability of handling a six-person camera crew,"

A sense of the rich and almost urban life that the team constructed for the atoll.

The entrance to Gregor's loft.

Gregor at work on a submersible, an early idea that didn't make it into the finished film.

The bar/trading post in the atoll.

said Chesney. "Sites for camera setups were everywhere. The catwalks weren't meant to accommodate thirty people, of course, but if the weight were distributed properly, an additional ten people could be safely added. All the upper walkways were designed to handle about fifty pounds per square foot. We built them light enough so that we didn't sink the whole atoll, but strong enough so that walkways didn't collapse. When we were nearly finished with construction, we had an architectural engineer walk through it for over a week making notes to see if we'd missed anything. We wanted to make sure that in the atoll's wild maze of pipes we didn't fail to get enough support in some area. His only job was to look at high walkways and staircases, and he came back with only a few things that we needed to add here or there, mostly small stuff. Overall, we discovered that we had done a really good job. We had a lot of disguised handrails everywhere, too." The walls of the atoll reached an average height of nearly thirty feet with four different levels inside; the watchtower levels, the upper catwalk level, the interim habitat roof levels, and the lower water level. Several architectural points, such as the windmill on Gregor's tower, measured over fifty feet.

A society so completely dependent on the ocean for survival would naturally turn to fishing as a key industry. After the Mariner negotiates the front gates of the fortress, he glides past the fishery, built on F-2, and takes

"The atoll was once more prosperous than it is today," noted Klassen. "It is, in fact, dying. I liked the idea of showing death visually, which was why we designed the shark to hang in front of the fishery. It's dead, it's been picked clean, and the people are coming down to the very last portions of it—just like the atoll. The shark had the look of a hammerhead to a certain degree, but it had ribs like a whale. We decided that if the earth had changed so radically, the whole ecosystem of the fish might have changed as well—just like society. The Atollers are in a state of decay. They no longer have any kind of trust in human nature and their structure as a society reflects that. I think the element of death is pretty significant."

As he makes his way further into the atoll, the Mariner sails past a funeral taking place on the Organo Barge, built on flotation number eight. "There was a whole theory behind every section of the atoll," commented Klassen. "With the Organo Barge, we wanted an Asian flavor because in China, for example, they grow food for millions of people in very little space. We decided that that kind of productivity reflected the Atollers as well, so we made a kind of rice paddy/Organo Barge where they grow all their plants and vegetables. Film is not a three-dimensional medium. It's a two-dimensional medium, so it was essential to create depth on film. We designed the sets with that in mind, building in layers so that we could get the depth and texture we wanted on screen."

While not the heaviest set, the Organo Barge was the largest in diameter and the last one to be built. It was designed with three very different levels in mind. A dying lemon tree, representing the Tree of Life, was at the top. The next level down offered a combination food-growing area and cemetery, complete with headstones. The bottom level featured the organic sludge that was made up of dead bodies and recycled waste. The Organo Barge was basically a liquid compost heap and burial ground used to return nitrogen and soil nutrients to the atoll's very poor soil. In reality, the set consisted of a giant tree made of wood, plastic, and foam with a steel structure built inside for support. An L-shaped sludge tank contained a 3,000-gallon mixture of sawdust and a biodegradable food thickener called methyl cellulose.

After the Mariner passes the Organo Barge, he swings his boat around and docks in front of flotation number three—the assay office—which was actually the fourth flotation barge to arrive and begin set construction at Kawaihae. The assay office is where the Mariner trades the valuable dirt he carries for chits—the plastic coin of the realm—which allow him to do business at the trading post. "The assay office was one of the smaller sets," noted Klassen, "but it *did* present certain logistical problems because it was also the narrowest. That gave it a very high center of gravity, with the capability of tolerating only a very low weight. We had to redesign the assay office set several times. We ended up making it wider because at first it

> "I liked the idea of showing death visually, which is why we designed the shark to hang in front of the fishery. . . . It's been picked clean, and the people are coming to the very last portions of it."

failed every one of the tests that Lockheed did in the tank with the atoll model. Every time they did a wave test, it would turn. We changed it by redistributing the weight and making it about twelve feet wider overall."

While walking to the trading post the Mariner passes the manufacturing plant, which was built on flotation number four. In this recycled society, the manufacturing plant reworks plastic into new materials, as with the gates. "We're saying that in this world," explained Nancy Haigh, "plastics float to the surface, where they're skimmed up and poured into a vat and then molded into new shapes. Basically this is a real possibility; up until recently most plastics didn't biodegrade, although plastics companies have been working on it. In Waterworld, the recycling plant uses plastics and their by-products to manufacture items that are needed by the Atollers. They manufacture the sheets of plastic that make up the exterior wall of the atoll. They also make the segments that connect the different sections of the atoll together. We're saying that the reason *this* atoll has evolved from looking like a group of boats strung together into a floating city with fortifications is because the people who live there have come up with a way in which to transform recycled plastic."

The factory set was intended as a reflection of Gregor's genius, for in the story he is credited with coming up with the concept for the intricate system. "Gregor has created the factory," explained Klassen. "He is the Leonardo da Vinci of his day. He has been able to harness the wind for electrical power, and devised a system of gears that accomplish a variety of things. They contribute to grinding the plastic down with special wheels that go around on top of the one main disk. Other cogs run the bellows, which feed the heat melting the plastic into the crucible. The molten plastic is then poured into all the different molds. A picture's worth a thousand words, and the factory really showed the ingenuity of Gregor and the Atollers."

The Mariner then walks to the trading post and tavern, which are located on the two flotation barges that are connected as if one—F-5/6. There he obtains the most precious item in Waterworld—drinking water, called hydro to distinguish it from the abundant salt water on which they live. Because this is a dying atoll there are only minimal items for trade, and along with a pure grade of hydro, the Mariner ends up with a scrawny

"Gregor is someone who pieces together clues from the past and uses them in an inventive way," observed Michael Jeter. "I think he is someone who is held in esteem by his fellow Atollers because he has done estimable things, but at the same time he's found very peculiar. People find him absolutely idiosyncratic and, in some ways, an outsider. He has a certain amount of power that he uses in a benign way, but he also uses that power to protect the people he loves."

tomato plant and the shelves from the store itself. It is here that Helen and Enola are first introduced. Helen, who tends bar and conducts the meager trade, also cares for young Enola, who wears a mysterious tattoo that has captured some interest among the tavern's patrons.

Attached to F-5/6 is the Chinese junk, which serves as the meeting hall

"Helen has a very unique relationship with Enola," said Jeanne Tripplehorn. "It's not the traditional mother–child kind of relationship. I actually looked at them as a couple of individuals who came together as survivors. In fact, I love the twist where the audience finds out that Enola is not Helen's child by birth—I didn't want that to be immediately apparent. Enola is an unusual, magical child and Helen is her protector. Helen is not an extremely maternal person, but she loves Enola and recognizes that she's very special. Enola holds the key to Dryland and, by protecting Enola, Helen is protecting that key."

The scope of the atoll construction may be best grasped in this view of the earlier stages.

for the elders of the atoll. The junk is the only wood structure on the entire atoll and represents a sacred place to the citizens and elders of the community. The wood of the junk is still intact but, like the rest of the atoll, it is deteriorating. "We fashioned the junk quite deliberately after a Chinese influence," noted Klassen. "We did a lot of research on Chinese architecture and boat design and were fascinated by the way they were able to capture a royal feeling so elaborately. We did have some difficulty with the set, however, because it weighed more. It was made out of wood and then covered in plaster, which made it very heavy. We couldn't use brand-new pieces of wood because it wouldn't have looked right. The plaster was used to make the wood look old and textured, but it had water in it, which created a lot of weight. We got into logistical problems because of that, but found ways to compensate. We changed the wood siding on the boat to foam siding. We made a mold and shot it out of foam, so it was lighter in weight. We also had to compensate for the beams, which were all made out of wood, but we managed to get the weight down and have it turn out looking just right."

Next to F-5/6 was flotation number seven, upon which was built the desalination plant and Gregor's Tower. The stockade was also attached to this flotation. The desalination plant—which removes salt from sea water—is another invention of Gregor's and an essential key to the survival of the society. F-7 was the first set the crew built, and it established a base for the atoll's resident genius to devise the numerous inventions used throughout the community. Described in the script as Vernesque—after turn-of-the-century French science-fiction writer Jules Verne—Gregor's workshop is a marvel of scientific exploration and ingenuity. It is equipped with a peculiar chairlike device that features two propellers attached to the back. A patched-together tentlike ceiling hangs above. Special-effects crews constructed a special four-point rigging suspension that would lift the chair toward the end of the atoll sequence, revealing that, in combination with the ceiling, it is an incredible escape balloon. A miniature of the balloon flying away from the atoll would be added later in postproduction.

Gregor's Tower was further equipped with a large windmill on top, making it the highest point on the atoll at nearly sixty feet. In the story, Gregor has designed the device to harness the wind and provide a crude form of electric energy for the little lights that sprinkle the atoll, while at the same time powering the plastic grinder in the factory. "The windmill and all its gears had to move and rotate," explained Peter Chesney. "The connections were a very big deal. It had a belt drive, a big steel axle, and its own little gas engine to turn the blades. The whole thing weighed about 5,000 pounds. It had a center shaft coming through that turned with big peg-style gear cogs—just like the inside of a clock. The tip of the blade was eighty feet off the water and the base of the windmill tower was forty feet high. It had a sail, and when the wind blew hard, the windmill would rotate to the wind just like a real working windmill because it had casters built in. There was canvas fabric stretched between a steel frame on the four blades and then it was painted similar to the trimaran."

Gregor's loft after opening to allow launching of the escape balloon, one of the creative vehicles designed to be used on and off the water.

During principal photography, two of the twenty-five tanks connected to the F-7 barge were removed to reveal the exceptionally beautiful water that shone through the mesh flooring of the set. The water of Kawaihae Harbor was such a stunning color—changing from aqua to deep turquoise to an incredible, vivid blue—that the filmmakers wanted to capture it during a segment featuring Gregor's Tower. By flooding the tanks with water, a team of scuba divers was able to lower the tanks to the bottom of the harbor during the shot. They were later hoisted, drained, and replaced beneath the unit.

"When I first saw the set and looked down into the water, it was beautiful," recalled Dean Semler. "And once we got inside the atoll, it seemed to be magnified in its beauty and color. The color was much more intense in there—partly because we were looking down through the muted steel set that surrounded it. We pulled out some of the tanks that were underneath Gregor's Tower in order to see the translucency of the water below it. There are a couple of shots in the movie where you can really see its wonderful opalescence. The color of the water changed from morning until afternoon inside the harbor; it was amazing."

The boat that Helen shares with Enola is located in the same section as Gregor's Tower. The interior is decorated with numerous charcoal drawings that Enola has rendered upon virtually every surface. The pictures reflect some kind of long-buried memory; images of birds, people, trees, mountains, and rivers are haunting reminders that she possesses a mystical connection to Dryland.

The final part of the atoll is the armory, F-9, which was actually the second flotation barge to arrive and begin construction on the Big Island. "F-9 was really the easiest one to make all the adjustments on," said Klassen. "It was the first unit we put our first boat on, and the first one we had to cut some of the decking from—so we learned a lot with that section. The armory is the area where the Atollers stash all the weaponry. When the Smokers are seen on the horizon, they go to the armory and get their weapons to prepare themselves for the attack. We designed catapults and huge crossbows, which were really quite spectacular. We equipped the Atollers with plastic balls that had shark-shaped teeth cast from plastic, along with numerous blades, spearguns, mallets, lances, and other primitive kludged-together weaponry." Property master

"Enola has thoughts about Dryland," said Majorino. "I think they are memories, but she doesn't know *how* she remembers them. She doesn't know what they mean. She draws different things from Dryland from a memory she can't remember."

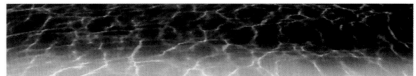

Michael Milgrom helped design many of the futuristic action props and was responsible for their construction and maintenance.

The atoll's eight separate flotation units were connected in a unique fashion to allow each one to move independently of the others. A shock cell, or knuckle, as it came to be called, was designed to join the sections

together securely, while providing optimum flexibility at the same time. The knuckles were made of steel pipes that were engineered to a specified criteria with rubber bushings inside that allowed the units to move ten degrees in any direction. That way, the filmmakers could achieve the desired wavelike motion of a boat on water, while at the same time guaranteeing the best structural solution to the problem of joining the eight separate units into the circular formation of the atoll. The centers of gravity and buoyancy so essential for safety were thus maintained for each individual unit. The designers had been concerned with a worst-case scenario in which a large wave might cause the boatlike structure to flip over. The flexible knuckle system guaranteed that if any particular section *were* to

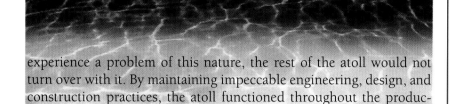

experience a problem of this nature, the rest of the atoll would not turn over with it. By maintaining impeccable engineering, design, and construction practices, the atoll functioned throughout the production with only minor repair requirements and no disastrous mishaps whatsoever.

Just as the safety of cast and crew members was a primary consideration during the atoll's design and construction phases, it was a chief concern during production as well. At least twenty water-safety crew members—from an overall crew of about a hundred—patrolled the atoll's lagoon in the event of accident or injury during principal photography, under the supervision of safety coordinator Alvin Tobosa. The crew was made up of off-duty firefighters, lifeguards, rescue divers, and others who paced the steel decks, ready for the first sign of trouble. "We stationed about two safety patrol people to a barge," said line producer Gene Levy. "They were all over the place, and whenever there was a cast member on the trimaran, we had two or three divers ready in the water. Two first-aid

people were on the set at all times, and there was a medical clinic only fifteen minutes away. With the sea of humanity we had on the atoll, we had to be very careful about possible injuries." A separate crew was responsible for constantly skimming the harbor, both inside and outside the atoll, to immediately pick up any debris that might have fallen into the water. Water tests were conducted weekly to make certain the harbor was not inadvertently contaminated by the production company, and all materials used were biodegradable. The filmmakers had pledged to return Kawaihae to its pristine condition at the conclusion of production, and were determined to fulfill that promise.

In coming up with the set decoration for the atoll, Nancy Haigh and crew followed the same logic established by Dennis Gassner and the art department. Lead man Robert Greenfield and assistant set decorator Paige Augustine, along with set dressers Mark Weisenfluh, Leslie Linville, Richard Anderson, and Jim Meehan joined Haigh in accomplishing the tremendous task of dressing the intricate futuristic sets. "We figured that there would be no wood in Waterworld," said Haigh, "and that different kinds of plastics and metals would survive. As a result, most of the items on the atoll were made up of those elements. Now, this was not a completely true situation—

we know that we *don't* know what's going to be around in 500 years. If we look back 500 years to the Crusades, for example, we have an understanding about what survives because items from that time are in museums. They vary in quality, of course, depending on the conditions and how they were taken care of, but we know that tapestries can survive, and so can wood. However, when you consider the effect that water has on these kinds of things, we don't really know what would happen. So we took some poetic license in figuring out what the people of Waterworld would have available to them. We decided that barrels and milk jugs and so on would float to the surface as available materials. We decided that the boats that made up the atoll—there were ultimately sixty or seventy boats built into it—would have been scavenged by the people who found them. That way we could justify sails and ropes and other things.

"We made all of the furniture—chairs, tables, cooking utensils, and so on—with the idea that they had survived hundreds of years and had been passed down. We also considered that certain items might have been found on boats, or that the fishing flotillas had netted them along with the fish. We learned about a place called the Sargasso Sea, which is a relatively calm area of water northeast of the West Indies, where, because of the way the trade winds all come together, it's like a giant garbage pit. If you were in an airplane looking down on it, you would see a huge collection of plastics and nets and buoys and trash that floats and collects there. We figured the Atollers would have access to something like this. We asked ourselves, 'How would the Atollers take all that stuff and make it useful again?' The answer was they would recycle everything."

Following the example of the Atollers, Haigh and her crew used recycled items to come up with the abundance of materials needed to establish the beautifully detailed set pieces. "When I was hired on the movie I was told I would need barrels, nets, and rope," noted Haigh. "But when I arrived in Hawaii the reality set in; I realized that sometimes the Atollers would need places to sit down and sleep and so on. I looked around for resources and realized that there weren't any. Here we were in Hawaii, surrounded by water, and I couldn't find any boat masts, I couldn't find any marine junkyards. It didn't make sense to me. Then I learned that there are actually fewer marinas in the state of Hawaii than almost any other coastal state in the union, because there are so few lakes, rivers, and streams. Therefore a marina becomes a very valuable piece of land. We did find a little marina down north of Kona and one on the other side of the island in Hilo—and Kawaihae did have a few boats—but that was it."

The first few months were frustrating for Haigh. As with the design and construction of the atoll, she had no precedent to follow in establishing the furnishings that would embellish the set. She returned to Los Angeles with an uncertain mission. "We knew we had to buy everything we were going to use," she said. "We couldn't rent anything because not only were we

"We asked ourselves, 'How would the Atollers take all that stuff and make it useful again?' The answer was they would recycle everything."

going to change it, we were then going to paint it, weather it, and expose it to the elements—so it wasn't like we could return things in any kind of acceptable shape. Our criteria was no wood and certain kinds of metals and plastics, but we also figured, 'Who knows what's going to float to the surface?' I was desperate, so we contacted all the prop houses and asked them if they had anything that they wanted to unload that nobody wanted to rent anymore. Three responded. They asked, 'Well, what do you want?' And I said, 'Well, I don't know what I want, I just want stuff.' One prop house in particular was especially helpful. They had purchased a container from an MGM auction years before and had it just sitting in their yard. They had never even opened it. They weren't going to do anything with it so they sold it to us with the provision that we take everything that was inside. It was wonderful. It was like going to a birthday party and buying a favor for a dollar, and not knowing what you're going to get. It was so amazing— and I bet we used just about everything in it. There were flats, there were banners from *The Ten Commandments,* there was medical stuff, airplane stuff, railroad stuff, car stuff. There were things in there from all walks of life. It was great because it was such a potpourri. We weren't always so lucky, but that was a wonderful treasure."

A few weeks later that same prop house called Haigh to inform her that they had decided to clean house and wondered whether she might be interested in more junk. Her response was emphatically affirmative. "It was a great way to find more items," she said. "There are prop houses for property masters, and prop houses for set decorators. There are also some that cross over, but this one was mainly for props. So I walked through the place just to see what I was going to get. A week later we sent a truck and got all kinds of terrific things. That was how it evolved; we just kept scrounging wherever we could.

"We packed everything into forty-foot-long Matson shipping containers and had them barged over from Long Beach. It took about two weeks for them to reach Kawaihae because they had to go through Honolulu. That's how we brought over everything we needed. On *Forrest Gump,* I brought one container from Los Angeles to South Carolina—we brought *eleven* over here. Then my gang, who's been with me forever, and a couple of people from Oahu started assembling baskets and chairs and lamps and tables and so on. Some things worked and some things didn't work; we just kept going."

Haigh also needed to provide the requisite miles of netting that had been originally requested. Obtaining enough appropriate netting created an additional challenge altogether. "The nets fishermen use today are almost like fishing *line,*" explained Haigh. "They're made of a really thin monofilament, which would never have read on camera. We realized that we needed to find the older style of netting, which is made of a nylon and cotton. We wanted it to look really ripped and repaired, sort of a patched-together look. There was a man in San Pedro who was really wonderful. He helped us a lot. He gathered nets from all his buddies in the San Pedro marine world and brought us 15,000 pounds of nets—that was seven and a half tons—which nearly filled an entire container. I thought in the beginning, 'There's no way we're going to use this,' but we ended up using nearly every bit. The atoll just ate everything. We'd put it out there and it ate it up."

* * *

Shooting on the atoll involved tapping all possible resources, as well. "I've described it to people as trying to shoot inside a giant Brillo pad," noted Kevin Reynolds. "There were so many different angles and sharp edges. The colors were all very monochromatic, as well—just blue water and the drab color we got from the rust and mold of the building materials that we used. That presented a problem because it was very easy to lose people on a set like that. They just didn't stand out against it. When you've got so many different angles, there's nothing that's particularly distinct—which is why I compared it to a Brillo pad. That created some problems with geography. The sheer size of the atoll created enormous problems as well. Since it was supposed to be out in the middle of an endless ocean, we always had to shoot with a clean horizon behind it. We were constantly try-

Shooting on the atoll involved tapping all possible resources, as well. "I've described it to people as trying to shoot inside a giant Brillo pad," noted Kevin Reynolds.

ing to find angles that didn't show the breakwater, and we couldn't shoot in the other direction because it would have revealed the entrance to the harbor behind us. So we had to plan our days around rotations of the atoll. We had to rotate it in the harbor and always shoot out to sea. That presented enormous logistical problems."

A marine department was established under the supervision of Ransom Walrod to coordinate the various tugboats, support craft, and picture boats—the vessels that would actually appear on film—used throughout the production. They were also given the tremendous job of moving the atoll.

Early on, the filmmakers had been required to go to the U.S. Coastal Trade Commission for licensing purposes in connection with the atoll, and discovered there was no set classification for the largest floating articulated structure in the world. So, to develop the design specifications necessary in marine engineering and naval architecture, it was determined that the atoll would be classified as an "unmanned vessel." That meant it could not be moved with people aboard. It also became clear that a captain of authority was needed. Billy Pupuhi was named atoll master and charged with the twenty-four-hour-a-day responsibility of supervising the atoll and all of its movements.

Extensive studies and calculations had been done to make certain the anchors and anchor chains were strong enough to hold the atoll to the mooring. Sixty tons of high-grade two-inch chain and nearly a hundred tons of anchoring held the 1,100-ton atoll safely in position. Understandably, moving it was no small task. Rotating it within the harbor took about six hours, and required ten people orchestrating a flotilla of motorboats and tugs to coordinate the unwieldy system of ropes, chains, and anchors. Divers worked underwater using airbags to float the anchors up and shift them to a new site on the bottom of the forty-five-foot-deep harbor. Under normal circumstances, this was accomplished during the night to facilitate the arduous shooting schedule.

"Shooting on the atoll was challenging because we were only able to look in one direction—out to the horizon," observed Dean Semler. "And that limited us to approximately a hundred degrees of vision. But Kevin Reynolds had made sure the angles of the shots were all storyboarded, and they were very accurate. We always knew when we would see over the walls or through the gates of the atoll—which indicated the times when we needed to rotate it. There was generally a discussion at the end of every day as to where the atoll needed to be for the next day. Filming on the water was very difficult, and sometimes it was frustrating because we had very little control over the elements. But we stuck to the shooting schedule as best we could; it simply wasn't possible to wait for the perfect light or the perfect water conditions for every shot. In a film like *Waterworld,* you can't get too precious about your own department. *Everyone* had to compromise to get things done—and when it came together it was wonderful. Kevin and I had talked initially about an overall look for the film, but after a while it began to take on its own look. The design itself—the atoll and the wardrobe and the boats—is what really gave the movie its look."

3. WATERBORNE FOE

I tell you naught for your comfort,
Yea, naught for your desire,
Save that the sky grows darker yet
And the sea rises higher.

G.K. Chesterton

The offer might have tempted an ordinary man—but when the Mariner is approached by the grim-faced elders and asked to contribute his seed for the replenishment of the atoll's somewhat stagnant population, he politely declines. It seems a simple enough transaction, yet as he attempts to leave the Mariner has an unpleasant encounter with a gatesman and the gill behind his ear is revealed. He is instantly recognized as a despised mute-o. After an attempted escape, he is incarcerated and declared a public threat; the sentence is death by way of recycling. The Mariner is thrown into a cage and slowly lowered into the suffocating ooze of the Organo Barge. A large band of Smokers suddenly appears on the horizon—this time with their leader, the Deacon—distracting the Atollers from their strange justice and causing them to turn to the more immediate matter of defending their home against marauders.

The role of the Deacon had remained unassigned during preproduction while the filmmakers considered their options. As far as they were concerned, Dennis Hopper was at the head of a highly talented list of actors, but a previous commitment to star in a film for cable television had made him unavailable. By July, however, circumstances had changed. Hopper's schedule was determined to be clear during *Waterworld* principal photography and he was offered the part without delay. Hopper accepted and flew to Hawaii, where he immediately began filming.

For Hopper, *Waterworld* provided the opportunity not only to create a memorable screen villain, but also to reunite with some old and well-respected friends. "Kevin Costner and I basically started our careers together at Orion Pictures. Actually"—he laughed—"it was my third or fourth career and his first. Kevin was acting there at the time, and later on directed *Dances with Wolves*, which is one of my favorite films. I had also known Larry Gordon from before—we had both worked for Roger Corman at American International Pictures back in the sixties—and he's produced some really great pictures through the years. When I heard they were going to make *Waterworld*, I knew it would be a noteworthy project, and something that I certainly wanted to be involved with." With credits that included *Rebel Without a Cause*, *Giant*, *Cool Hand Luke*, *Easy Rider*, *Apocalypse Now*, *Blue Velvet*, *River's Edge*, and *Speed*, Hopper would bring his impressive and diverse range to the portrayal of the Mariner's most formidable foe.

Filming on the atoll continued throughout the summer and fall of 1994—both within the sanctuary of Kawaihae Harbor and on the open sea

due west. Scenes that took place early in the film—most notably the Mariner's arrival at the atoll and the ensuing Smoker attack—were finalized in the script and plugged into the location shooting schedule. Certain elements of the story, however, remained nebulous. Screenwriter Joss Whedon visited Hawaii and worked with Reynolds, Costner, and Gordon to finalize the script. Ultimately, he gave the epic its definitive spin— enriching characters, toning up relationships, and crystallizing story points to the satisfaction of all concerned.

Kawasaki provided state-of-the-art jetskis that were modified with fiberglass engine heads and fins to suggest futuristic decay.

Just as erecting the atoll had proven a hard-fought venture, so was staging the elaborate battle sequences that were filmed there. Numerous "picture boats" representing the Deacon's armada—as distinguished from offscreen support craft—were featured throughout the sequence, preparation of which commenced well in advance of the filming that began in June. Jetskis, Waverunners, and a single-wing, single-engine Helio Courier seaplane were properly corroded to reflect the Smokers' sea-ravaged decay. Effects were planned and executed by special effects supervisor Marty Bresin and his crew of more than 100, with stunts performed by a veteran team of stunt people coordinated by R. A. Rondell.

The Smokers' attack begins with a scout plane leading a trail of ragtag conveyances to the outer wall of the atoll. A floating ramp is towed into place and the more insane Smokers, called Berserkers, fly over the wall on skis and crash into the inner sanctum of the floating city. "It was a very complicated sequence," explained Rondell. "There were *so* many things involved with it. We had jetskiers racing around firing automatic weapons. We had boats that were firing automatic weapons and exploding. There were Waverunners speeding along throughout and ski jumpers were flying up over the walls of the atoll and landing inside. It was a very busy sequence."

Rondell spent considerable time with professional jetskiers, water-skiers, and Waverunner operators to prepare for the elaborate stunt work. "It was important to see what professionals were using for ramps in their shows and competitions," he noted. "Then I did a lot of tests with them—prior to my stunt team arriving in Hawaii—to make sure we were on the right track. Based on our research of professional ramps, we were able to design ramps that would accommodate both ski jumpers and jetskiers. I got a lot of positive and negative input from both groups about what we needed to do, and we continued to fine-tune everything throughout all the stages of testing. Two ramps were built for the movie. They could be adjusted from four feet off the water to ten feet, and measured about thirty-two feet in length and fifteen feet in width."

The free-floating ramps were made of steel frames placed on catamaranlike pontoons that could be moored or towed by boats to the desired position. The ramp bases had to be especially stable to support the arduous stunt work that would take place there. "We knew that a catamaran

The Hellfire Gunboat leads the attack, flanked by Smokers.

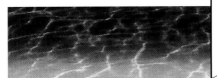

would provide the most reliable support," explained Peter Chesney, "but there weren't any catamarans that fit the bill in Hawaii. Hawaii is not a very big state in terms of industrial stock. It has an ocean all around it and bays here and there, so there are a lot of Windsurfers and small boats—even very big boats—but not much in between. The marine department built a catamaran from scratch in ten days—hulls and everything. They were pushed for time, but they did a great job. The problem was, it only went about eight miles an hour and plowed the water. They went to Bruno Belmont, who realized there was too much hull behind the outboard motor, which caused a pressure zone in the back of the hull. So he cut the hull off and tapered it up. After that the ramp boats would go about twenty-five miles an hour." Along with the ramp boats, several ladder boats were devised for scaling the atoll's walls—much as ancient intruders might have invaded a medieval fortress. Speedboats were fitted at the front with ladders that folded backward across the deck, with just enough room left over for screaming Smokers to pile in alongside.

In the film, the Smokers' scout plane pulls the water-skiing Berserkers up and over the wall of the atoll. The effect was actually accomplished in several carefully edited cuts and required the aid of a helicopter piloted by Craig Hoskins, who also flew the seaplane featured throughout the film. The helicopter pulled the water-skiers up the ramp at about fifty miles an hour and then lifted them into the air. Other shots, filmed separately, punched in the Smokers' frenetic landing within the atoll. Second unit director David Ellis worked with Hoskins and Rondell in capturing the image. The team devised a procedure wherein a steel bowling ball was suspended about 100 feet beneath the helicopter. Tow ropes were attached to the ball, which kept the loose lines safely away from the rotors of the helicopter. After the skier flying up off the ramp had been captured on film, the stuntperson would then get into a special chairlike rig, be lifted up once again, and jump into the water from a reasonably low level on the inside of the atoll. A similar shot featured a water-skier coming over the wall and crashing into the Mariner's cage. For that, a 500 foot rope rig was attached to a 200 foot crane and positioned above the wall. The stuntperson was then lifted over the wall and all the way across the water, past the top of the gate towers on the opposite side of the atoll. A pair of pulleys allowed him to slide down the rope as if he had been launched.

Kevin Reynolds knew that he wanted the effect of the Berserkers coming over the wall to have the same trajectory as a thrown rock. The effects and stunt crews approached his request scientifically. A high-powered

water-balloon thrower and a radar gun were obtained, and tests were done to determine the speed profiles of a water balloon coming over the wall in precisely the same manner. The match between the balloon and a human going over the wall turned out to be surprisingly accurate; each sailed over at almost precisely the same rate. In the end the effect worked like a stage punch, with the stuntperson flying past the towers and stockade—and missing the Mariner's cage by about four feet.

The Smokers' attack scene took four days to shoot. A special hydraulic rig was devised by the effects department to support Kevin Costner's prison cage while slowly lowering it in and out of the Organo Barge's methyl-cellulose-and-sawdust ooze. All the while, Costner remained stoically behind the steel bars. "It was a very difficult scene," recalled Michael Milgrom. "It was tremendously slippery there on the set. People were slipping and sliding and falling from seven in the morning until seven at night. We also had the biggest box-office draw in the world up to his ears in green slime—not a situation many other movie stars would put themselves in. The man was literally covered up to his ears with this stuff. Kevin kept getting dunked, but he was a real sport about it."

During the confusion of the attack, Helen and Enola approach the entrapped Mariner with a desperate proposal. If they free him from his rapidly approaching doom, will he take them with him in his escape? Without a better option, he acquiesces and Helen quickly snaps the lock on his cage. Helen and Enola slip through the chaos toward the gates of the atoll as the Mariner dives into the lagoon. He swims for the dock and emerges like a dolphin to wrestle his trimaran from the Smokers. Skillfully, he hits the levers that initiate the transformation sequence and—in the sailing mode once again—the trimaran is maneuvered toward the gates as Smokers and jetskiers run amok.

The twenty-eight jetskis and Waverunners that were used during the attack on the atoll—and throughout the film—were state-of-the-art models modified to suggest a look that was at once futuristic and decayed. Lead sculptor Fred Arbegast created fiberglass engine heads with motorcyclelike fins that were glued onto the sides of the housings. The effects department further modified the jetskis by transforming the old *internal* exhaust system into an external one, thus maintaining the notion of the kludging—or retrofitting—modifications the Smokers would have made. Furthermore, the designers knew the Smokers would have had smoky engines—as opposed to the environmentally correct, underwater exhaust systems of the 1990s—so the exhaust was rerouted to spew into the air instead. A reservoir and pump were added, with vegetable oil flowing into the hot exhaust near the engine and creating billowing smoke. The smoke system was rerouted to move it away from the watercooler, performance parts were added to increase horsepower, and expansion chambers were installed to embellish noise levels.

Fuel for the jetskis—and the multitudinous additional craft in the Smoker fleet—was provided by the Refueler Barge, the Deacon's command post and his largest and most significant conveyance. It is from this vantage point that the Deacon directs all maneuvers by way of young signal boys using flags. The Refueler Barge was built on the hull of an old Navy landing craft and equipped with a large bladder—used to store thousands of gallons of an unspecified, futuristic fuel—on its deck. The bladder measured approximately twenty-by-forty-five feet and was obtained at a military surplus auction on Oahu. Earlier designs had conceptualized it as being towed in the water behind the barge, but that had proven both logistically impractical and difficult to photograph. Instead, the eighteen-by-twenty-five-foot air bladder, which was made of nylon and then painted with latex to create a rubberized effect, was carried on board the vessel. It was then pumped full of air to simulate the fuel that powered the Smokers' crude and varied armada.

The Hellfire Gunboat was another key element in the Deacon's armada and represented his most powerful weapon. After the machine gun–equipped jetskis and Waverunners have prepared the way, the Hellfire Gunboat—manned by Smokers and the Hellfire gunner—blazes through as the ultimate show of force during the attack on the

atoll. "The Hellfire Gunboat is the jewel in the Deacon's crown," commented Milgrom. "It was equipped with four .50-caliber machine guns firing—at least hypothetically—'*Deez*-made bullets. It was sent out to decimate anything in the way of the Deacon's armada. It wasn't really a boat, but rather a barge that measured about eighty feet in length. It was motorized by a Mack truck connected to an enormous gear-driven paddle wheel system that powered the back. It looked something like a gambling boat going up the Mississippi River." The paddle wheel was made of a rubber bumper with chained-on tires. A belt was removed from the truck's rear wheels to drive the paddle wheel, while another belt drove the cranks that powered the guns.

The Hellfire Gunboat's four machine guns were built on vintage World War II assault mounts manufactured by Hechler and Koch, and were capable of firing 600 rounds per minute. They functioned like real guns, but discharged cardboard wads coated with waterproofing—as opposed to the more familiar blanks traditionally used for theatrical purposes. Use of the machine guns, along with various other rifles and pistols, was supervised by first unit weapons specialist and armorer Dan Sprague and second unit weapons specialist Harry Lu, both of Stembridge Gun Rentals.

The Hellfire Gunboat represented only a fraction of the firepower employed throughout the film. The Smokers were equipped with numerous other weapons, used extensively during their attacks on the Mariner and the Atollers, which required the considerable involvement of Marty Bresin and his special effects team. "On a heavy effects day we averaged about 3,000 bullet-hit effects," noted Bresin. "That meant 3,000 squibs, zirc balls, sparking granule balls, and dust capsules. It wasn't unusual to have between six and eight guys with guns shooting continuously." Effects teams also monitored dozens of smoldering tins filled with charcoal briquettes and frankincense that laced the labyrinthine paths of the atoll and filled the air

with ambient smoke during battle sequences.

The elaborate battle sequences shot on and around the atoll required exhaustive preparation and painstaking choreography on the part of Bresin and crew—so much so that he found himself turning to a few longtime friends for assistance. "We did an incredible amount of pyrotechnics for *Waterworld.* This movie was so large that I actually put out some calls to friends and took advantage of their good will. For instance, Chuck Gaspar came to Hawaii to work with me—Chuck's done most of the Eastwood movies and *Ghostbusters,* just to name a few of his films. Joe Mecurio, who's probably done hundreds of movies, also came over. Eric Rylander set up and dispatched the big pyrotechnics we did on this show, and he's one of the best pyrotechnicians in Hollywood. We also had Ralph Kerr—our resident engineer—who helped me design all the gags. Then, of course, there was Dale Ettema, my assistant coordinator, who ran the show with me. Dale took charge of all the personnel and hired the people we needed for the various sequences. For instance, the scene where the machine guns on the Hellfire Gunboat are blasting away at the atoll was the start of the big attack sequence. It was a huge job, and we needed a really large crew and a lot of preparation. We had 1,200 bullet-hit effects along the atoll that used primer cord explosives to blow eight-inch holes in the side of the atoll. And that was just one shot! It started on one side of the atoll and went across nearly 300 feet of simulated machine-gun fire. It was an incredible scene, but then the whole movie was incredible. As far as I know, we had the largest special effects crew ever put together for a film. We had as many as 154 special effects technicians—and I think that record will stand for a long, long time."

In the confusion of the attack, the Mariner—having tripped the gates' counterweight system—begins to clear the entrance of the atoll in a voluminous spray of water. It seems he has no intention of taking on as passengers the woman and child who aided his escape, but Helen and Enola leap to the trimaran's deck as it passes beneath them nonetheless. The Mariner steers the trimaran toward the open ocean at full sail, leaving the burning atoll behind. The Hellfire Gunboat is behind the Mariner as the Deacon and company signal for the gunner to blast the trimaran out of the water. The Mariner harpoons the Hellfire Gunboat and spins it around with a length of rope as the gunner continues to spray everything in his path.

Water-skiing Berserkers are pulled over the wall of the atoll by the Deacon's scout plane. The elaborate stunt was meticulously choreographed by stunt coordinator R. A. Rondell and team, along with helicopter pilot Craig Hoskins and second unit director David Ellis.

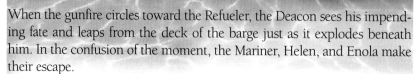

When the gunfire circles toward the Refueler, the Deacon sees his impending fate and leaps from the deck of the barge just as it explodes beneath him. In the confusion of the moment, the Mariner, Helen, and Enola make their escape.

"Blowing up the Refueler Barge was a really big effect," said Bresin. "We had to plan it very carefully. First, Eric Rylander and I discussed it thoroughly. Then he came up with a plot plan—a schematic—of exactly where each explosive went and how much of it was needed. Altogether we launched about twenty-five fifty-five-gallon barrels into the air, and used nearly 700 gallons of gasoline, along with a *lot* of primer cord and sparks. It was a huge explosion."

As always, safety was a primary concern whenever gunfire or explosives were used during production. Standard union safety procedures were strictly adhered to and the company's daily call sheet alerted cast and crew members whenever weapons would be fired. Additionally, the actors were carefully instructed as to the appropriate use of all weapons by the Stembridge crew, who also made sure the guns were impeccably maintained. "We used earplugs and face masks whenever guns were fired," said Milgrom. "We did the same thing whenever there were big explosions. We put blankets on top of people if they were in close proximity to gunfire, and tried to use the lightest load of ammunition possible, while still achieving the effect the director wanted. Running the battle sequences was a very serious endeavor, and we didn't take the responsibility for the safety of our people lightly."

Keeping people safe was equally imperative to R. A. Rondell and his team of stunt players. "We rehearsed the stunts very thoroughly before the cameras ever rolled," said Rondell. "In fact, there was a *lot* of rehearsal time on *Waterworld*. We walked everybody through the areas they were involved with and made them aware of different obstacles that might be in their way. A safety supervisor was on hand at all times, and the crew was responsible for letting us know if they noticed anything sharp or unsafe. Sometimes we highlighted areas with fluorescent paint so that people could see what was involved prior to filming. If areas had problems, they were immediately fixed. Whenever there was a fall we set up pads or boxes called 'catchers'—although a lot of people fell into the water, which made it easy. I personally swam the atoll many, many times underwater, making sure it was clear below the waterline, with no dangerous obstructions sticking out. It was built so beautifully that it was very clear off the sides and in the water, but we had to make sure all the mooring lines were properly marked so we knew where they were if we had to do falls into the water."

Another essential aspect, both within the battle sequences and throughout the film, was the abundance of weapons and other props. Created under the supervision of Michael Milgrom—who worked along with assistant prop master Ken Adachi and prop crew members Eric Fishman, Scott Anderson, and Ralph Reiss—props for *Waterworld* numbered in the tens of thousands and required twenty-five weeks to prepare. "My department was responsible for the action props," explained Milgrom, "the things that people could hold or shoot or drive. There were easily over 10,000 individual props in the movie, including 5,000 arrows, another 500 shark-toothed spears, about 300 rubber and real machine guns, another 100 handguns, and at least 500 shark-toothed spear balls. We had to manufacture and maintain all of them." Because of the vast numbers of props required, and the necessity of creating exact duplicates for many of them, Milgrom called on several Los Angeles–based companies to work along with the *Waterworld* staff during various stages of manufacturing. "Because we needed so many duplicates, we had to have quite a few of the props manufactured," he said. "But much of the work was done by our own shop people. Fred Arbegast sculpted the models for all the weapons, and did a beautiful job. I would bring him an original piece that I had found and we would discuss how it needed to be rusty and where we might want to add some kind of leather roping to give it a kludged-together look. Then Fred would make a model and a mold and our manufacturers would pour them in rubber. On some of the props, we added a steel bar inside to keep them from bending and to make them look real on camera. Our head painter, Pat Gomes, did terrific

Gerard Murphy as the Deacon's chief lieutenant, the Nord, stands ready with a futuristic weapon.

finishing work, embellishing them with the correct amount of corrosion and aging."

Working along with Dennis Gassner and the art department, Milgrom helped design many of the props, as well. "Coming up with all the props was such a big job that sometimes I would wake up in the middle of the night dreaming about it. Part of it was probably the insomnia of the tremendous task I had ahead of me, but I think some of it was inspiration. I actually came up with some of my ideas during those long nights. Kevin Reynolds had some very specific ideas as to the look of the guns. He wanted it to seem as though the Smokers had taken 500 years of junk parts and put them all together to build a weapon. A 9mm rifle clip might be added to the barrel of a shotgun, for instance, with the ammunition clip from a .50-caliber machine gun. He wanted them to look cobbled together. So I went out and found a lot of great real guns and started adding separate pieces to achieve the look he was after."

Milgrom also took into account that, on the set, the weapons would be handled by a great number of people, resulting in a certain amount of unavoidable damage and loss. "One of the biggest lessons I learned on this film was that we could design a lot of great stuff, but unless we made it practical, it wasn't going to hold up for more than a day. We also had to make many of the pieces functional. Crossbows really needed to fire arrows. Machine guns really had to shoot—and they had to shoot in a lot of situations around corrosive water. Salt water is terribly hard on metal and ammunition. And yet we were in a situation where water was very prevalent and guns *had* to fire. It was a difficult situation at best. Our armorer, Dan Sprague—and all the people from Stembridge—did a terrific job cleaning the guns with solvents and oils every day to make sure they didn't corrode or rust."

* * *

During July and August, the atoll remained snugly anchored within Kawaihae Harbor, where filming progressed within a gangplank's reach of land. By early September, however, the company had completed all the principal photography scheduled within such comforting proximity, and the time came to venture seaward. Ransom Walrod and the marine department

Prop master Michael Milgrom—working along with Dennis Gassner and the art department—designed a variety of kludged-together weapons for the Smoker arsenal following Kevin Reynolds's notion that the guns look like centuries of pieced-together junk parts.

choreographed three tugboats that pulled the over 1,000-ton atoll a half mile west where it was anchored at a depth of ninety-six feet. Anchors had been disconnected in the harbor, and a large anchor was set, along with several buoys, prior to the arrival of the floating city—which took the better part of a day to reach its location. The atoll was then firmly moored at the center. Thus removed from the constrictions of the harbor, it could be rotated easily on the ocean's frictionless surface whenever necessary.

The deeper water possessed the same unnatural beauty as Kawaihae Harbor. "The water was incredibly clear out there," said Bresin. "If you put on a snorkel and mask, and floated on the surface, you could actually see the bottom. I personally went down to fifty-three feet and saw octopus, coral, and fish. The crew and I fed schools of tropical fish right out of our hands—they were so tame you could feed them with your right hand and pet them with your left hand. We had a thirty-foot whale shark that adopted the atoll. Divers were actually able to go right up and pet him. We even saw groups of six- or eight-foot mantas mating nearby. It was incredible; it didn't look real. It didn't look at all like a movie set."

Out of respect for the sanctity of their surroundings, the production company maintained a crew of divers whose sole task was to clean the ocean floor. Personnel equipped with skimmers maintained the surface of the water, just as they had within the harbor setting. Furthermore, a local marine laboratory was charged with making certain that porpoises were nowhere near the atoll, or in any of the surrounding water, whenever explosives were going to be used.

For Dean Semler and the camera department, filming on the open sea presented an untold number of new challenges. "We had come to Hawaii in March to do some tests with rigs and mounts and Steadicams," recalled Semler, "so we were as prepared as we could possibly be. We quickly learned, however, that no matter how prepared we were, our shots depended entirely on the seas. We could plan for ideal conditions, but if the ocean swelled or the wind came up—and sometimes we had ninety-mile-an-hour winds—there was nothing we could do. Lighting the actors was one of the biggest challenges, especially on the trimaran. On land you have full control. You can put up scrims if the sun is too cruel, or you can introduce large lights if you need to fill from one side or the other. You can replace the sun with your own lights. Out on the ocean it was a different matter. Instead of having two or three 12,000-watt lights through giant frames to soften the light on the actors—as you would on land—we had two or three *1,200*-watt lights. That made it difficult. Scrimming the actors seemed to work reasonably well on the trimaran because we had a lot of rigging and could fly scrims, but then if the wind came up, it would become a problem. In fact, wind caused all sorts of difficulties because, with the sails up, the trimaran could only sail in a certain direction. That influenced the way we could shoot. We couldn't say, 'Let's turn the trimaran and sail this way.' The trimaran had to go with the wind."

The problem of lighting was one Semler had to contend with throughout production. "Lighting was tricky because the design of the whole picture was so drab—which is what it *had* to be. In *Waterworld*, there were no primary colors, no rich colors at all. It was all the khaki-drab colors of old fish skins—the set, the wardrobe, and the boats. It became very difficult to have principal characters stand out in any way. It's very easy to position someone on a highway against a brilliant blue sky and get some dynamic composition. It was more difficult in this film, particularly on the atoll, because everything blended together. We put hundreds of extras out there and we couldn't see them. They just disappeared like camouflage. If the light was flat, everything tended to blend in. We used lights and lenses the best we could, and backlighting and smoke helped pull the characters out a bit, but it was still tough."

Under ordinary circumstances, maintaining visual continuity between shots would have been a fairly routine matter. Matching the quality of light, or the appearance of the water and sky, for example, is generally an everyday aspect of the camera department's job. In *Waterworld,* however, these abundant elements shifted and changed almost constantly, and matching exact water and sky conditions between takes was more than an artistic indulgence; it was an impossibility. "The color of the water changed from pale green to almost black, depending on where we shot and the time of day," said Semler. "The intensity of the sun varied considerably, as well. In the morning, the sun was directly behind us, the sky was a deep blue, and the sea was a rich cobalt blue. As the day went on, the sea got darker. When the sun came up over the top of the actors at midday—and we had to be careful about the shadows under their eyes, and so on—the water would turn almost black. In the afternoon, of course, we had backlighting, and the water became silver-hot and reflective. We finished up every afternoon looking into this exploding, white-hot reflective backlit sea—and there was nothing we could do about it; we just had to keep shooting and working around it. Logistically, it was impossible to even attempt to cope with that kind of lighting problem. But we weren't there to shoot a schedule for art's sake; we had to adhere to a schedule for a zillion other reasons more important than that. We weren't allowed the luxury of matching water and light conditions—it simply wasn't possible. And yet, somehow, it all worked out. We had the same situation with the *Mad Max* films, where we had to shoot through all different light conditions. We learned that if your heart's in the story, and you're tuned into the drama, those kinds of things don't even matter. The same held true for *Waterworld*."

The Hawaiian sky posed the same kinds of challenges. "I loved that island," continued Semler. "The sky went from white to rich blue to fabulous clouds. It was like *Ryan's Daughter* country, just extraordinary. The skies were different every day. But once again, we couldn't spend time trying to get a continuity of the sky. We generally shot with the drama of the story, and trusted that the audience wasn't going to worry about it. There were times when, if we started a sequence in backlight in the afternoon, we'd come back the next afternoon and try to pick it up, but mostly we just plugged away, sticking to the schedule as best we could and capturing the story on film."

An early Stefan Dechant sketch of a Smoker handgun. Because so many guns were required for the film, scores of duplicates were manufactured in Los Angeles based on molds created by lead sculptor Fred Arbegast.

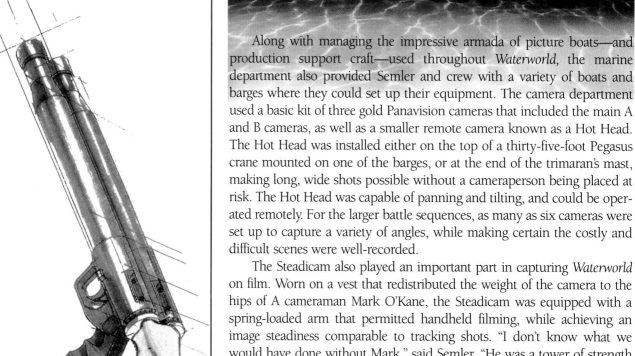

Along with managing the impressive armada of picture boats—and production support craft—used throughout *Waterworld*, the marine department also provided Semler and crew with a variety of boats and barges where they could set up their equipment. The camera department used a basic kit of three gold Panavision cameras that included the main A and B cameras, as well as a smaller remote camera known as a Hot Head. The Hot Head was installed either on the top of a thirty-five-foot Pegasus crane mounted on one of the barges, or at the end of the trimaran's mast, making long, wide shots possible without a cameraperson being placed at risk. The Hot Head was capable of panning and tilting, and could be operated remotely. For the larger battle sequences, as many as six cameras were set up to capture a variety of angles, while making certain the costly and difficult scenes were well-recorded.

The Steadicam also played an important part in capturing *Waterworld* on film. Worn on a vest that redistributed the weight of the camera to the hips of A cameraman Mark O'Kane, the Steadicam was equipped with a spring-loaded arm that permitted handheld filming, while achieving an image steadiness comparable to tracking shots. "I don't know what we would have done without Mark," said Semler. "He was a tower of strength and stamina, and wore that Steadicam all day long as he bounced up and down on the open ocean. He did an extraordinary job. We also had some incredible grips—guys who ran around doing a little bit of everything. We had them all over the place—up in the air in cranes and climbing up and down the masts of the trimaran. We even had them underwater. They did underwater training and put up scaffolds and towers and rigs below the surface. We had, as a minimum, nine grips working, and even more on certain days."

Underwater photography was accomplished under the supervision of Peter Romano, who filmed on location in Hawaii during the summer and fall, and in a special tank at the McDonnell-Douglas Aircraft Corporation after the production company returned to California in December. B camera operator Richard Merryman was responsible for capturing surface shots of surf riders and various craft passing overhead during principal photography off the shore of the Big Island. Merryman used a camera equipped with a special housing that enabled him to film on the surface of the water. "Richard worked on the *Mad Max* films with me," said Semler, "so he had a good feeling for the dynamics and angles of action. He did a lot of surface-water camera shots of the jet-skis and trimaran passing over him. His camera just sat on the surface while he rode a pink rubber giraffe—one of those kids' toys you blow up for putting in the pool. Richard would just float out there with his camera, waiting for his shots."

* * *

Principal photography continued at sea until mid-November, as well as on stage in the sugar shack, where interiors of the trimaran and 'Deez were captured on steadier ground. The atoll remained moored just west of the island, and was moved from its anchor only three times during the shoot, with its first relocation dictated by some indisputable weather concerns. On the morning of October 4, an alarming, but never life-threatening, tsunami struck the Kona Coast of Hawaii. Just as *Jurassic Park*'s Kauai shoot had been shut down by the arrival of Hurricane Iniki in 1992, Mother Nature took similar control during the filming of *Waterworld*. "We were listening to the tsunami warnings on the news at 5:30 that morning," recalled Marty Bresin, "and by the time we got to work at 6:00 for our safety meeting, a siren started going off—one of those old civil defense sirens I used to hear as a kid. Then we started getting reports on evacuation and the fire department came down and said they'd like everybody to evacuate by 9:00, since the tsunami was supposed to be here by 10:28. The evacuation was very orderly; everyone went up the hill toward Waimea. We stayed until we had wrapped everything that could get wet, and either covered or moved the rest of the gear up to the sugar shack. We moved all the vessels—including the atoll—out to six hundred fathoms of water because the tsunami had no effect at that depth. The entire harbor was void of ships for a few hours." The entire incident was over by the end of the morning, and the *Waterworld* crew returned to work that same day.

The atoll was moved a second time in late October, when it was returned to Kawaihae Harbor for a week of repairs. Welds on the mammoth structure had been weakened by some exceptionally heavy seas, and workers labored to render it satisfactorily sound. It was returned to its original offshore mooring site for a few more weeks of filming, until finally, in mid-November, the atoll was towed back to the harbor for the last time.

It was Thursday, December 8, when the *Waterworld* cast and crew wrapped the five-month Hawaii shoot. The complexity of the production and the challenges of facing the impetuous sea had proven immense. Understandably, the production schedule had been extended far longer than anyone had initially anticipated. "We learned a lot as we went along," commented Dean Semler, "but if we went back now, it would take just as long to shoot this film. We did what we had to do out there on a day-to-day basis—and I don't believe we could have shot it any faster or any better. Making *Waterworld* was always challenging, and sometimes damn near impossible. But it was a remarkable experience—and we did it."

4. SEA COLORS

ostumes for the inhabitants of Water-world were based on the same logic that drove the rest of the film's design—the reality of a futuristic world of subsistence on the open sea. To John Bloomfield, this made perfect sense. He appreciated that there would be limited resources available in such a world, and understood that a life of desperate deprivation would bear some kind of social impact. Certain elements, like the sun-bleached hues and weathered fish skins of the color palette, were obvious to him from the beginning. Other aspects of the design were more elusive, and required a process of investigation and experimentation. To help define a look for the costumes, Bloomfield had met with Kevin Reynolds on Easter Island while they were still in production with *Rapa Nui,* and the director had offered some general guidelines for *Waterworld.* That gave Bloomfield a foundation to work from, but when he went home to England at the end of 1993 a tremendous task still lay ahead—the design and construction of more than 2,000 original costumes for one of the biggest epics ever filmed.

"I just sat on my own in England all through December doing drawings and panicking," he recalled, laughing. "I started the project in sheer terror. Then I came to Los Angeles and spent a few days talking about the look of the film with Dennis Gassner. I really wanted to avoid anything too stereotypically futuristic, which was a most difficult thing to do. It would have been so easy to make the costumes look stupid. We were dealing with a time 500 years in the future, but I didn't want them to look anything like *Star Trek*, for example, and I was trying to avoid *The Road Warrior* look, as well. It was important for me to find my own way, some place between those two worlds. I started by thinking about the essentials and what these people would have had available to them. Obviously the whole idea of fish skin came up. As an extension of that, while reading and thinking and wondering what to do, I discovered that the Eskimos use walrus or seal gut—the intestine—which they dry out and cut into long, thin pieces of what looks like see-through silk. That discovery was directly applied to the costumes for the atoll elders. The long coats and robes they wear during the beginning of the film in the burial scene came directly from the Eskimos. Eskimos, of course, are faced with the same sorts of problems as the Atollers—they need clothing and have very few resources at hand."

Bloomfield was also aware of the atoll as a religious community. "When the Mariner first enters the atoll, he sees a ceremony taking place. The burial, with the priests and the elders, has obvious religious overtones. They also seem to be very hierarchical as a society. That made me think about the pilgrim fathers and the *Mayflower*, which is why they wear those big puritanical hats. The Atollers' costumes were really a combination of Eskimos and the *Mayflower*."

Dennis Gassner's designs for the atoll had also reflected a medieval influence, a consideration duly noted by Bloomfield. "When you look at the atoll, it's reminiscent of a medieval castle, as though you come over a brow of a hill in medieval France and see it. I also thought—because the Atollers have such a simple, highly organized society—about the Amish, who are simple farmers. Many of my designs for the Atollers were classic Amish, with high pants, suspenders, and flat hats."

Despite the Atollers' harsh existence and make-it-do reality, Bloomfield saw no reason to create costumes that were conspicuously unattractive. He believed they could maintain the gritty, futuristic world the filmmakers had established, while at the same time reflecting a pleasing aesthetic. "There seemed to be no reason to make these people look ugly. I wanted to create something that made sense storywise, but I also wanted to design clothes that were, in their own way, beautiful. As it turned out, everybody—the actors and extras—loved the costumes. They told me I should have done an actual line."

Bloomfield established an office at Universal Studios during the first part of January 1994. As he continued the intensive design work, he also began to assemble the crew that would help create the numerous costumes required by late spring. By the end of the month, he had hired Nick Scarano as costume supervisor. "Nick ended up doing an absolutely incredible job on the film," said Bloomfield. "Between the two of us, we started putting the show together. Greg Mowry joined us a little later on. He was basically responsible for cutting the costumes and was just great." Also assigned to the *Waterworld* costume department were assistant costume designer Chrisi Karbonides, key costumer Tony Scarano, and costumers Barbara Gordon, Katina Kerr, Daryl Athons, and Kathleen Felix. Specialty costumer Laura Baker, specialty wardrober Phyllis Thurber, and set costumer Brenna Charlebois were hired later on to assist with the costuming aspects associated with production.

During the initial design phase, Bloomfield found himself coming up with costumes for unknown players. With the exception of Kevin Costner as the Mariner, none of the roles were yet cast during the early days of preproduction, and Bloomfield was faced with projecting onto the characters impressions culled only through initial drafts of the script. It was essential to complete the design work in order to begin making the thousands of costumes needed by the beginning of principal photography.

"In a way, this sort of movie was based upon archetypal characters," he observed. "And it wasn't too hard to figure out the types. I knew Helen was going to be a beautiful girl who was tough and feisty. She wasn't going to be somebody who was weak or heavy or slow to move; they simply weren't going to ask anybody of that type to do the part. The Atollers were desperate people at the end of their rope. They didn't have any resources left to them; they're dried out, desiccated. The whole poignancy of the story is that this is the last atoll. So I knew the actors and extras playing the Atollers would, overall, most likely be spare. The Smokers, on the other hand, with their philosophy of 'live for today and there will always be another atoll to rob tomorrow,' would clearly be a different type. I knew they would be big and tough, and possibly even heavy. So when I started drawing, I took all those things into consideration. It was

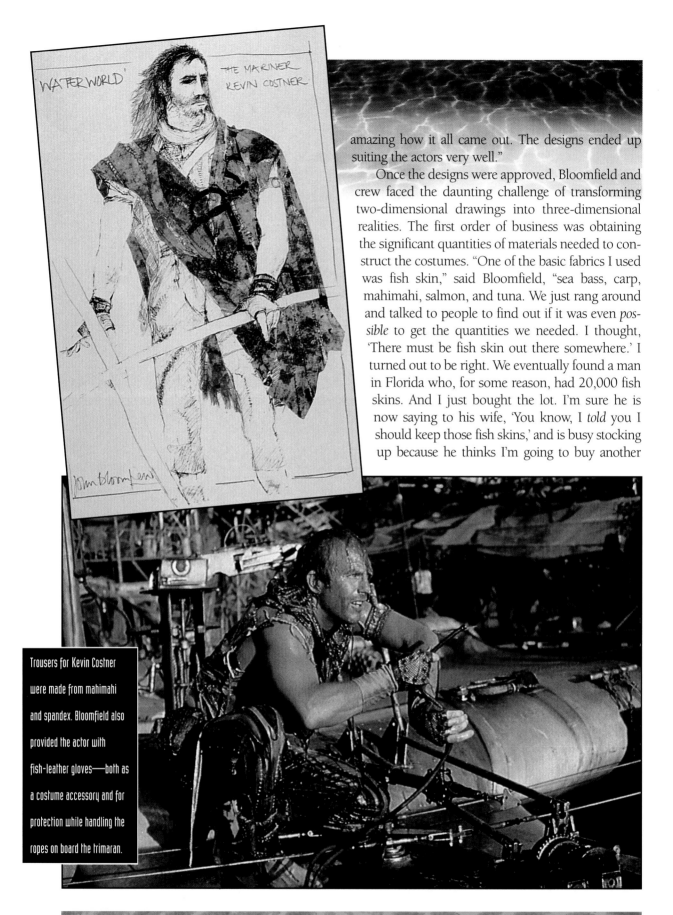

WATERWORLD · THE MARINER KEVIN COSTNER

John Bloomfield

amazing how it all came out. The designs ended up suiting the actors very well."

Once the designs were approved, Bloomfield and crew faced the daunting challenge of transforming two-dimensional drawings into three-dimensional realities. The first order of business was obtaining the significant quantities of materials needed to construct the costumes. "One of the basic fabrics I used was fish skin," said Bloomfield, "sea bass, carp, mahimahi, salmon, and tuna. We just rang around and talked to people to find out if it was even *possible* to get the quantities we needed. I thought, 'There must be fish skin out there somewhere.' I turned out to be right. We eventually found a man in Florida who, for some reason, had 20,000 fish skins. And I just bought the lot. I'm sure he is now saying to his wife, 'You know, I *told* you I should keep those fish skins,' and is busy stocking up because he thinks I'm going to buy another

Trousers for Kevin Costner were made from mahimahi and spandex. Bloomfield also provided the actor with fish-leather gloves—both as a costume accessory and for protection while handling the ropes on board the trimaran.

20,000. The truth is, I'll never buy another fish skin in my life."

Bloomfield also devised an artificial version of the Eskimo-inspired animal intestine he had discovered during early research. "The actual intestine was really gorgeous, it looked like silk. So I made an artificial version of this material *out* of silk. I bought silk organza and dipped it in plastic paints so it took on a natural texture. It looked exactly like the fabric the Eskimos made. It was, however, a bit expensive and also slightly fragile. We made some beautiful clothes right at the beginning and they were lovely, but I

Dozens of duplicate costumes were painstakingly made as replacements due to the wear and tear that took place during the strenuous shoot.

The Deacon's costumes reflected basic Smoker logic, but were embellished to suggest the diametrically opposed influences of Idi Amin and the Pope.

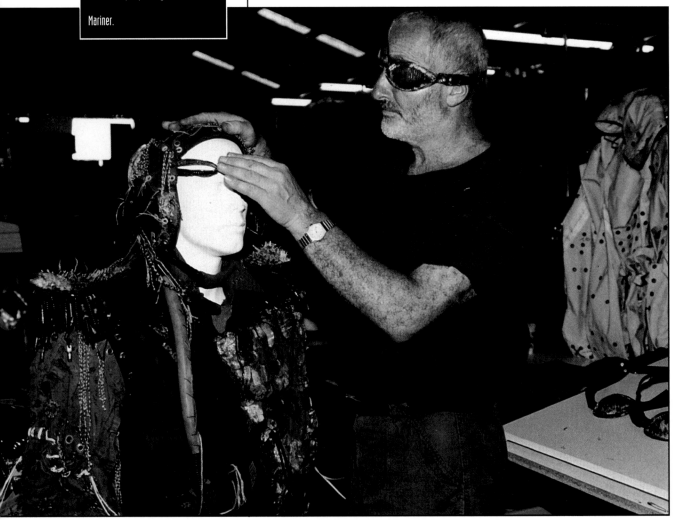

thought, 'These aren't going to last a week.' So we came up with a good alternative. I had gone out when I was looking for Smoker stuff at all the secondhand military establishments and found a man who had mountains of old rip-stop parachute nylon. I bought a truckload. It was much tougher than the silk organza, and it sandpapered up nicely—the sandpaper caught the texture of the rip-stop and pulled it to really nice shapes. It could also be dyed and painted very easily. We didn't have any trouble with those clothes; none of them collapsed at all."

In designing costumes for the Smokers, Bloomfield established a look that was the antithesis of the Atollers. "I wanted the Smokers' appearance to be instantly frightening and instantly strange. Everything I came up with for the Smokers was always in direct opposition to the ways in which I thought about the Atollers. I knew it was going to be quite monochromat-

John Bloomfield makes an adjustment on the Deacon's eyepatch. More than a costume accessory, the eyepatch was dictated by the script after the character loses his left eye doing battle with the Mariner.

ic on the atoll, with everything very natural and tied into the sea. I wanted the Smokers to be shocking. As they came out of the smoke during their attack on the atoll, I wanted a very dramatic effect. I dressed them in the most shocking colors I could think of: black, red, yellow, and orange. I also felt that those same colors were very easily derived from natural rusts and organic processes; I absolutely avoided any blues, or colors that were obviously touched with a chemical dye process. It was a false solution, really, but that was the way I looked at it. You create a reality when you're doing something like this and you have to stick to the rules of that reality. I also figured that the Smokers might use remnants of old plastic bags and things they had discovered in the bottom of the *'Deez.* I didn't think many people would be able to read in their community, so when they'd find old sacks of dangerous pollutants and toxic waste,

The Deacon's coat was fashioned after a biker's leather jacket, but modified to include spring-laden epaulets and genuine blowfish on the shoulders. As with other key costumes, several exacting replicates were manufactured by Bloomfield and crew.

they would think they were looking at the Dead Sea Scrolls. I simply started drawing and thinking in those directions."

Costumes for Kevin Costner's Mariner followed a similar course of thought. Bearing in mind the character's ability to dive and scrounge from long-lost cities, Bloomfield knew the Mariner would surely discover treasures without any comprehension of their origin. Various touches were added to his costumes in support of this notion. In an amusing nod toward the conspicuous consumption of present-day society, the Mariner wears—like a mythic warrior's armband on his bicep—a gold Rolex. "We bought a dozen fake Rolexes to use throughout production," Bloomfield said. "We had to have duplicates in the event of damage or loss. I figured that the Mariner would have found the Rolex in a jeweler's shop window in Denver when he was swimming around down there. He didn't quite know what it was for, but it was a nice piece of jewelry, so he put it on."

Over the Mariner's shirt, Bloomfield modified an old yachting jacket that had been ripped apart and pieced back together as a vest. "I wanted

the vest to look as though it had gone all rusty and old," he explained. "You could still see a bit of the logo—a little sail and the letters 'U.S.' The colors were really beautiful. We washed it and washed it so the oranges and blues were less apparent, and it ended up in jewel tones of turquoise and soft orange. His trousers were made of mahimahi, with some Spandex added so they had a little give. We painted them with subtle shades of green and brown and turquoise,

which made them look slightly iridescent and wet—as if he'd just come from the sea. I was really nervous about those trousers at first because I thought they might be a bit too heavy, which they had to be in order to hold up. They ended up working great, however; Kevin loved them and said they were really comfortable. The pants went in and out of the water with no problem— we made sure to oil them every day to keep them in good shape. The hardest part was having to make fifteen identical pairs. It wasn't just a question of cutting and sewing more pants, we had to match the fish skins and design in *every* detail." Customized carp-skin boots were made for Costner, and Bloomfield further equipped him with fish-leather gloves, both as an intriguing costume accessory and as protection for the actor's hands while managing ropes aboard the trimaran.

The Deacon's costumes were even more detailed. They reflected basic Smoker logic, but were further embellished when his character was described in an early draft of the screenplay as a combination of Idi Amin and the Pope. Bloomfield actually obtained a photograph of the Pope, taken at the Vatican in October 1978, and a similar shot of Idi Amin to use as reference points; his own imagination took the Deacon's costumes the rest of the way. "You need to make costumes look interesting and authentic," he commented, "but it's very easy to become too complicated and go over the top—and then they don't look real. There's a fine line between making something realistic, while also making it look unusual. This was the case with the Deacon. Like the rest of the Smokers, he has discovered relics from the past and interprets them in a way that makes sense to him. He doesn't know what on earth they *really* are, of course, but he uses them in a way he understands—as religious artifacts of sorts."

Part of the Deacon's costume featured an elaborate shawl, not unlike the kind of sacred vestment the Pope might wear. "We covered his shawl with items that were recognizable to us," said Bloomfield, "like all kinds of bottle

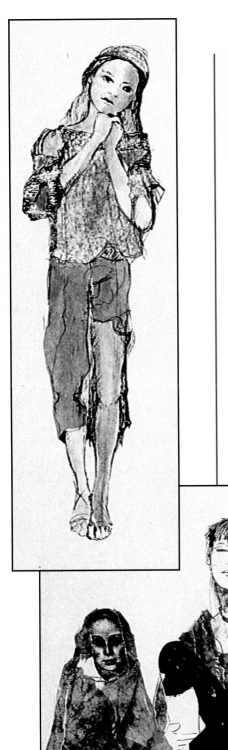

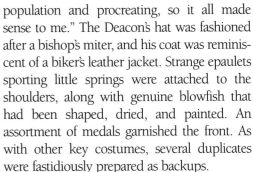

caps. That also tied in with the Idi Amin influence, because they looked like strange sorts of medals. There were bits of radios, perhaps suggesting his powers of communication, along with other little odds and ends we could find. It also seemed as though he was involved in some sort of baby cult—he has those little flag boys who work for him and he very purposefully captures the boys from the atoll. So we found some dolls at dime stores, smashed in their faces, and attached them to the shawl. As a final touch, we came up with Band-Aid boxes containing little dolls for him to hang on his back, much like Catholics used to carry around boxes bearing the remains of saints. I think he reveres babies—I don't know if it's because he loves them or eats them—and the Smokers seem to be into overpopulation and procreating, so it all made sense to me." The Deacon's hat was fashioned after a bishop's miter, and his coat was reminiscent of a biker's leather jacket. Strange epaulets sporting little springs were attached to the shoulders, along with genuine blowfish that had been shaped, dried, and painted. An assortment of medals garnished the front. As with other key costumes, several duplicates were fastidiously prepared as backups.

Along with his megalomaniacal leadership tendencies, the Deacon also happens to be a golf enthusiast. In support of this intriguing layer of characterization, Bloomfield created customized shoes for Dennis Hopper. "I looked around and there were necessities everyone had to have," said Bloomfield. "The Deacon had to move, he had to cover his feet, and he had to be comfortable. He needed shoes and they had to be tough. We found some very plain Adidas shoes that covered our criteria perfectly, and then we embellished them to look like *Waterworld*'s interpretation of golf shoes."

In creating costumes for Jeanne Tripplehorn's Helen, Bloomfield followed the same design criteria that had been established for the Atollers while evoking a look that was decidedly more romantic. One of her costumes was a dress of what appeared to be crocheted kelp, over which she wore a fish-skin bodice. The medieval-style bodice was complete with reinforced eyelets, called grommets, through which laces were fastened in front. "I made a huge amount of work for myself when I started using grommets on this film," admitted Bloomfield. "I thought it was such a good idea that I incorporated them not only into Helen's designs, but into *many* of the others. I thought they would look great—and they did—but it turned out to be a *lot* of work. We used a hand machine and must have used millions. I really developed quite a muscle, just grommeting up the costumes on this show."

For Enola, the mysterious child who scribbles plants and waterfalls on every surface within reach, Bloomfield created clothing that reflected this artistic obsession. He made sure her dress was covered with drawings similar to those rendered by Tina Majorino on camera. "I had Tina come in and do some sketches for me," he said. "That way I knew

what her style was. Then I copied them onto her costume using waterproof felt-tip markers, so they didn't come off in the water. The dress was lovely, but really quite fragile because we made it from real silk. We knew from the start that it wouldn't last throughout the entire shoot, so we made a total of ten identical dresses for her. After we had been filming for about a month it became clear that even ten dresses wouldn't be enough. So we made twenty more just like them."

Michael Jeter's character, Gregor—the inventor/wizard of the atoll—wore a coat made entirely of patched-together fish skins and other accessories that reflected his unique personality. "The patchwork looked so wonderful, but re-creating and duplicating it was hard work," said Bloomfield. "It wasn't just a matter of cutting out a piece of fabric. We had to match up all the fish skins and, oh God, it took forever! Of course, for Gregor, we also had to attach all sorts of gadgets. He had a whole different variety of looking glasses—from monocles and lorgnettes to little binocularlike things. They hung all around him because he was always examining things. For the night sequence, he wore a marvelous hat that looked something like a windmill. It actually lighted up."

The costume for Gregor, the inventor/wizard of the atoll, was made of patched-together fish skins—a time-consuming proposition considering that several exact duplicates of the costume were mandated by the production.

Hats for the other Atollers were equally unique and different, with every one reflecting the reality of Waterworld. "I had about four hat people working for me," Bloomfield said. "Some of the hats were made from basic cane structures; others were made of silk to look like translucent fish intestine—those used small pieces that had to be pieced together. Another idea was to have them look a bit like lobster pots. We just made the cane shapes and then painted them with vermiculite to give them a bit more texture. In one case, the script specifically mentioned the elders wearing jellyfish hats. Well, what does that mean? In looking around for a suitable material I discovered rawhide—which is just the uncured inner lining of leather—that we could soak and maneuver into any shape we wanted. So we started making really interesting hats out of that. The rawhide was very durable, as well."

Costumes for additional characters, such as the doctor, the depth gauge guy, and the Smoker families were equally well conceived and detailed. The flag boys, who served the Deacon as signalers from the Refueler Barge, wore black and yellow costumes made of knitted cotton that were painted to look like old plastic wire knitted together.

*   *   *

Beyond clothing dozens of principal actors and extras with the appropriate Waterworld accoutrements remained the considerable task of creating and applying equally accurate makeup and hair effects. It was clear that a climate born of harsh sun and endless water would strongly affect the appearance of the people who lived there, and the filmmakers appreciated the importance of establishing this on film. The job of rendering sunburned bodies and weathered faces fell to makeup supervisor Frank Perez who, along with assistant makeup supervisor Jim McCoy and a legion of professional artists, made sure the characters of *Waterworld* maintained, through makeup, the reality that had been established so meticulously for the film.

Perez' and McCoy began by meeting with Kevin Reynolds to discuss the director's expectations for the film's makeup. "Kevin had some pretty specific ideas about what he wanted the characters to look like," recalled Perez. "For the Atollers, he wanted a very weathered, tanned, overexposed look. That made perfect sense for people who lived their lives on the open sea. He wanted the Smokers and Berserkers to look very greasy, grimy, and

Wearing a hat that lights up by virtue of a miniature windmill, Gregor visits the Mariner, who sits entrapped within his Organo Barge prison.

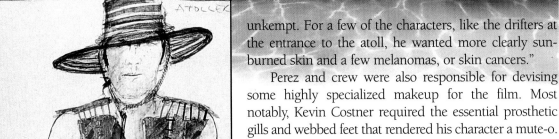

unkempt. For a few of the characters, like the drifters at the entrance to the atoll, he wanted more clearly sun-burned skin and a few melanomas, or skin cancers."

Perez and crew were also responsible for devising some highly specialized makeup for the film. Most notably, Kevin Costner required the essential prosthetic gills and webbed feet that rendered his character a mute-o. Dennis Hopper needed prosthetic makeup as well, when the Deacon loses an eye during the attack on the atoll. "Besides all that," said Perez, "we had to deal with face and body makeup for hundreds of extras each day and *water-proof* makeup for all the people going in and out of the water. We also had to make sure little Enola's tattoo was accurately applied every single time. I don't know what I would have done without Jim McCoy. His experience really made the show run smoothly. As with every other department, *Waterworld* was a *very* big movie."

To design and sculpt the essential prosthetics for the Mariner and Deacon, the filmmakers called on veteran

The elders of the atoll officiate at a burial on the Organo Barge. The long coats and robes worn by the elders of the atoll in this scene were inspired by the translucent walrus intestine used by Eskimos. The elders' jellyfish hats were actually made of rawhide.

special makeup effects artist Tom Burman who—along with his wife and longtime partner Bari Burman—was responsible for developing the various appliances used throughout the film. They began by developing the gills that would define the Mariner as the mutant creature so abhorred by the Atollers.

Costner's feet were similarly created, with Burman sculpting and casting webbed appliances that fit the actor precisely. Perez made soft acrylic spreaders that were placed between Costner's toes to hold them gently apart, and a thin membrane of latex skin was applied from the top of his feet to the tips of his toes. The webbed feet required approximately forty minutes, per foot, to apply, and offered the realistic appearance Kevin Reynolds was looking for. The gills required a

A Smoker in full costume.

similar application time for each ear, while Costner's straight makeup, applied daily by Perez, consumed a mere twenty minutes.

To show the considerable facial injury and eye damage suffered by the Deacon when the Refueler explodes, the Burmans sculpted a series of three different appliances for Hopper that connoted the progression of the wound and its treatment. For the scene in which the doctor attempts to replace the Deacon's missing eye with a large, painted ball bearing, a special prosthetic was devised to permit the "eye" to fly out when Hopper turned his head. The appliances were applied by makeup artist Fred Blau, Jr., who painstakingly placed stitches over the "cut area" on Hopper's brow with black string to enhance the realism of the illusion. Although time-consuming, the effect was extremely convincing. In all, Hopper spent about an hour and a half in the makeup chair prior to filming. To simplify matters, he wore an eye patch fashioned from an old goggle whenever the story line permitted.

While Frank Perez and Jim McCoy attended to the principal actors, makeup artist Jeanne Van Phue readied the featured performers and Fred Blau, Jr., supervised makeup for the remaining Atollers and Smokers, who represented the majority of Waterworld's inhabitants. With impressive efficiency—and at least two hours and an army of sixteen makeup artists—makeup was applied en masse to scores of stunt players and more than 100 extras every day.

Boasting a core group that numbered in the hundreds, and ranging in age from six to sixty-five, the extras were fundamental to

the reality of the futuristic world. Extras casting director Tammy Smith had conducted two open casting calls—one on the Kona side and one on the Hilo side of the island—earlier in the spring and interviewed nearly 6,500 people for the variety of available parts. Under the direction of Kevin Reynolds, Smith followed his guidelines of seeking out those bearing a gaunt Amish or puritan look, while at the same time being open to a diversity of ethnic backgrounds. "Kevin Reynolds was very involved with the hiring process," noted Smith. "Actually most directors are; it's a crucial part of setting the mood for various scenes and really bring- ing the story to life. But Kevin was particularly meticu- lous about it, more than any other director I've ever worked with. It was especially important for this pro- ject because we were working in a contained area, on the atoll, with a large ensemble of people that rep- resented a community. As it turned out, the people we hired created a wonderful community of their own while working on the picture. They were really great and gave a lot to the film."

Virtually all the Atollers required full body makeup, and a three-sided wooden spray booth was set up next to the harbor to facilitate the assembly-line process. Water-based pancake makeup, tinted with the appropriate sun- baked tones, was sprayed onto players, who then reported to the large shed where makeup artist Carol Borden and crew completed their work with finishing touches of grime and sunburn. "When you have that many people," said Blau, "you have to expedite. We put the makeup in a regular spray gun, hooked up to air compressors, and sprayed everybody down. After the spraying, we pointed up their faces so they didn't have a flat look. We had to model them out a bit and add a little sunburn stipple to their faces." The Smokers went through the same procedure, but were covered with a darker brown makeup and smudged with grease and oil effects instead. After getting into wardrobe, all the extras then reported to hair supervisor Elle Elliott; key hairstylist Janis Clark; and hair- stylists Sue Maust, Patricia Budz, and Linda Sharp, who teased, sprayed, and powdered their contemporary locks into futuristic disarray.

Bloomfield wanted the Smokers' appearance to be instantly strange and frightening—shocking colors and unnatural textures were chosen accordingly.

For the stunt players and actors who would come in direct contact with water, there was an entirely different problem to solve. The water-based makeup that was spritzed on the majority of performers so successfully would quickly dissolve after a frantic jetski ride or dive from the trimaran. "We had to have a makeup that would hold up when performers were out on the water," said Blau. "We knew we wouldn't have the opportunity to touch them up—it would have been logistically impossible. So I thought about it and came up with a waterproof makeup that really held up in water. I made it especially for this show and it was the first time it had ever been used. It was formulated with an ink derivative—like the kind used in movie tattoos—and an alcohol base to which resin pigment was added. As the alcohol dried, the pigment adhered to the skin." Uncertain as to whether or not his formula would be successful, Blau began by trying out a couple of pints just to see what would happen. The results were so overwhelmingly successful, he ended up manufacturing it by the gallon, with up to ten gallons being used every week. As with the regular body makeup, the waterproof makeup was sprayed on and then stippled for texture. Different colors were also concocted to serve as waterproof cuts and bruises.

Removal of the waterproof makeup required a special formula to dissolve its resilient pigment. At the end of a long day of filming at sea, performers returned to clean up in rustic showers furnished with soap, shampoo, and solvent. "Removing the waterproof makeup was something like taking off an appliance," said Blau. "It needed a little help to come off. And because there were so many players, we had to use the same mass approach we used in the morning when the makeup was applied. When they came in after filming, we sprayed them down with the remover—which was really an oil-based solvent that broke down the resins in the makeup. They didn't need to scour at all. They just needed to let the remover saturate through the makeup and it washed off easily. Then they showered, shampooed, and went home."

Because of Blau's experience with cinematic tattoos, having created them in abundance for films such as *Tattoo, Illustrated Man,* and *Rising Sun,* he was naturally called upon to render the tattoo that would cover Tina Majorino's upper back throughout the film. He developed a tattoo stencil based on a design provided by the art department. The appearance of Enola's tattoo had always been clearly dictated by the script as an indispensable story point. Described in Peter Rader's original draft as partially intersecting dark and light circles, with a white line and a little triangular bump, the tattoo's design had evolved along with the story. "We always

Costume design for "Vulture," one of the Deacon's henchmen in an early draft of the script. The character—looking decidedly like a bird of prey—disappeared from the story in later drafts.

knew there was going to be an Asian feeling to the design," said illustrator Stefan Dechant, "because in the story the characters eventually end up on Mt. Everest on the Nepal-Tibet border, which made sense—it would have been natural for everyone to head for the highest ground if there were massive floods like the ones that created Waterworld. Dennis Gassner and I looked at oriental symbols, like the yin and yang and dragons, for example. We explored various ideas and discussed them with Kevin Reynolds. As it turned out, he knew very specifically what he wanted. He handed us a four-by-five card with a circular shape that displayed land on top with an arrow pointing toward it, and a few Chinese characters alongside to indicate longitude and latitude. Kevin felt very strongly about that image because it fit directly into the revised script. So we took his drawing and crafted it into the tattoo. We tried to be as accurate as possible with the characters because, in Chinese, the style of every stroke is very important. The lines of the tattoo had to be thickened a bit so they would register on camera, but all in all, we did very little to alter it. Enola's tattoo was really designed by Kevin Reynolds."

Once the tattoo's design was completed, Blau duplicated it onto a silk screen, from which hundreds of newsprint stencils were made. The stencils were then transferred onto Majorino's back with alcohol, in a manner not unlike the transference of colorful Cracker Jack tattoos onto the arms and legs of children.

5. UNDER WATERWORLD

From the great deep to the great deep he goes.
Alfred, Lord Tennyson

To the denizens of Waterworld, the bounty of the sea is boundless. It is upon water that they build their homes; from water that they draw the basic elements of survival; and through water that they define their understanding of the world. It is without beginning and has no end—beyond water there is, quite simply, more water. But while the breadth of Waterworld is traversed as a simple matter of course, the depths remain an unquestioned mystery. Below the surface lie danger and darkness, and without a means of drawing life-giving oxygen, few humans would consider anything more than superficial exploration.

The Mariner, of course, sees things from a different perspective. Equipped with gills and webbed feet, he is able to endure long stays beneath the ocean, and the underwater world is as familiar to him as the surface. Not long after he escapes the burning atoll with Helen and Enola, the Mariner reveals his amphibious gifts by patching a hole in the trimaran's hull while underwater. Later scenes show him fishing for dinner—from *inside* an enormous futuristic fish—and, most poignantly, taking Helen on an underwater tour of the submerged city of Denver. The impressive underwater sequences featured throughout *Waterworld* were achieved by way of visual effects under the supervision of Micheal McAlister or live-action footage captured by underwater director of photography Pete Romano—and frequently as a combination of both.

Director of photography Dean Semler and director Kevin Reynolds pause between takes on the atoll.

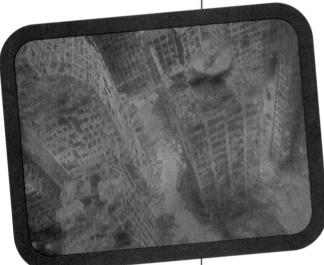

A view descending to the underwater city of Denver.

The Academy Award–winning McAlister came to the production with a well-deserved reputation for excellence after having spent eleven years at George Lucas's premiere effects house, Industrial Light and Magic, where he supervised visual effects for such films as *Indiana Jones and the Temple of Doom, Starman, Willow,* and *Indiana Jones and the Last Crusade.* His more recent efforts included *Die Hard 2* and *The Hudsucker Proxy*—all told, a wealth of experience that served him well in facing the new effects challenges presented by *Waterworld.* "We did nearly 350 visual shots for *Waterworld,"* said McAlister. "It was a huge job that represented some of the more innovative work that's ever been accomplished. We created computer-generated images above water and underwater, bluescreen composites, miniatures, wire removals, telescope point-of-view mattes, matte paintings, and even a small handful of optical effects. Some of the biggest challenges involved computer-generated water and underwater bluescreen work." Working alongside McAlister was veteran visual effects producer Kimberly Nelson, who had also worked at ILM and offered an impressive special effects background, as well.

The live-action underwater camera work also posed some unique and exhaustive challenges. Like McAlister, Romano came to the project with a strong background in his area of expertise, having served as an underwater cameraman for the U.S. Navy, and as a photographer on dozens of motion pictures, including *Navy Seals, Free Willy, When a Man Loves a Woman, Ghost in the Machine* and, perhaps most notably, James Cameron's *The Abyss.* For *Waterworld*—the most elaborate and ambitious underwater work he had done so far—Romano also provided the highly specialized lighting and camera equipment required for the film.

Because of the unique open water and underwater filming conditions, specialized waterproof equipment was essential. Romano and his company, Hydroflex, supplied *Waterworld* with cinematic tools capable of withstanding the demands of surf and submersion while remaining completely safe when exposed to the hazards presented by the combination of water and electricity. To do this, special waterproof housings were designed and manufactured to protect the camera and lens. Lighting equipment was similarly safeguarded. "Our underwater housings have worked on a number of shows," noted Romano, "but we also developed a lot of equipment expressly for *Waterworld*. The demands of filming on the ocean were considerable, and this was the most ambitious 'water' film ever. Dean Semler had some very specific needs for filming on the trimaran, the atoll, and out at sea—and there were also requirements for underwater photography."

All underwater camera housings were equipped with a special "video-to-surface" linkup that permitted Kevin Reynolds and Dean Semler to view above water exactly what the camera was seeing beneath. Communication was further facilitated by an underwater speaker system that employed a microphone and an amplifier. The filmmakers could then speak directly with the submerged cast and crew members, who could easily hear them within a fifty-foot range. Hand signals were used to reply, along with Romano's "nodding camera" technique that signaled, via video, either yes or no to the director above. "You find that if you're on the surface, everybody can talk about a shot for hours," observed Semler, "but if

Storyboards detailing the complicated sequence where Berserkers fly over the wall of the atoll and into the Mariner's cage, as he sinks slowly into the ooze of the Organo Barge.

Shot 93.a
Angle up on Mariner in cage. We see smoker skier come in over Atoll wall.

Shot 93.b
Skier collides with Mariner's cage, and the both fall out of frame.

Shot 94.a
Mariner's cage and the dead smoker land in the Organo barge.

Shot 94.b
Mariners rolls his cage over , letting the smoker fall into the Organo goo.

Shot 94.c
Camera pushes in and over the dead smoker towards the Mariner.

Shot 95
Mariners POV: of dead Smoker sinking in the goo.

Shot 96
Mariner reaches out towards the dead smoker.

Shot 97
Mariner's POV: His hand reaches out and grabs the knife

Shot 98.a
Mariner pulls the knife in towards himself, and rolls the cage on it back.

to pick the lock with his knife. Camera lifts and pushes in towards the

98.c
era continues to move in towards the mariner as he works the lock with his knife.
rows a look off camera.

Shot 99.a
Mariner's POV: we see the smoker sink.

you're down in the water, there's nothing to say. It's either working or it's not working. Pete's a very fine underwater cameraman, and his signaling system was simple and efficient. It was an easy matter of asking questions like, 'Are you okay?' And he'd nod 'yes' with the camera, or back and forth to indicate 'no.' We'd ask him, 'How long?' and he'd hold up two fingers for two minutes, or one finger for one. It was all we needed to know."

Prior to principal photography, tests were done with Kevin Costner and Jeanne Tripplehorn to give everyone an idea of what to expect in terms of working underwater—how costumes and makeup would react, for example, and what the performers needed to know while acting in such an unfamiliar medium. They were also trained in underwater safety and breathing practices. Scuba equipment and oxygen tanks were clearly out of the question, yet any kind of sustained underwater cinematography would have been impossible without air. Additionally, Romano was so encumbered with camera equipment that the surplus weight and bulk of

Crew working in center of the atoll.

David Silva (second second assistant director) on the atoll directing extras.

scuba gear would have greatly impeded his cinematic efforts. As a solution, individual safety divers were positioned off camera with second-stage breathing regulators for Romano and the actors. The divers monitored them constantly, providing oxygen from regulators between takes.

While bravely participating in the requisite underwater filming, Tripplehorn found the experience less than appealing. "I wasn't really fond of filming underwater in the ocean," she admitted. "It was extremely confusing and disorienting down there—very surreal. I could see my setup beforehand and get an idea of what I needed to do, but once I got down there I couldn't see—and I couldn't breathe. It makes you panic a little when the breath of life is taken away. Kevin and I had to have absolute trust in the people holding our regulators. There were a lot of things to keep track of just being underwater, and, on top of all that, we had to act."

Much of the underwater filming was accomplished just outside of Kawaihae Harbor. Early tests had employed a barge that was stationed—along with several support boats for the camera equipment—in the forty-foot water, with a speed rail extension attached to its side creating a platform for the performers. "The early test was great," Romano recalled, "and everything was working fine except for one thing. Because the barge was rocking, the platform was rocking—which meant that as I was trying to film the actors, they were moving in and out of frame. It was awful. It became clear that we would have to do something special in order to get the shots in a controlled situation in open water—although the truth is 'control' and 'open water' are two ideas that don't mix. As a solution, we built a staging platform right on the bottom of the ocean floor."

A stable, thirty-foot scaffolding was erected, placing Costner and Tripplehorn about ten feet below the surface—deep enough to avoid the woes of bad weather and seasickness, yet reasonably accessible and safe. To neutralize the actors' natural buoyancy, and prevent them from having to fight the exhausting tendency to bob to the surface, weights were worn that rendered them a mere pound or two heavier than weightlessness, thus facilitating almost effortless movement along the platform. On other occasions, they slipped their feet into straps that held them stationary. Underwater filming occurred intermittently in Hawaii throughout the summer and fall of 1994, with Romano returning for some second-unit footage near the end of principal photography in February.

Underwater shot of an atomic submarine crashed in the middle of a major Denver boulevard.

In the film, the Mariner and his unwelcome guests get to know one another within the isolation of his somewhat battered trimaran. His initial inclination is to dispense with the superfluous ballast—Helen might have her uses, but the child will do nothing but consume valuable water—and pitching Enola overboard seems like a good idea. But Helen persuades him to the contrary and, before long, Enola begins to get under his skin. "The Mariner's relationship with Enola really develops throughout the movie," noted Tina Majorino. "It has a beginning, a middle, and an end. At the beginning, she knows that she has a connection with him. Enola is different from the other Atollers and she knows how the Mariner feels because everybody thinks he's different, too. In the beginning the Mariner doesn't like her at all, and at the end he likes her a lot. I think he starts to like her because he begins to understand what she's like. They end up forming a very special bond."

Part of that bond is forged through adversity, as the trio suffers an assault by the Deacon's scout

plane, which descends on the trimaran with a spray of bullets. In an effort to defend their craft, Helen fires a harpoon line from the Mariner's heavy gun, which happens to be attached to the bowsprit. The line links the trimaran to the scout plane, and the harpoon stand, having torn free from the deck, becomes lodged in the spreaders of the mast. The scout plane circles the trimaran, winding the line dangerously around the mast, in a visual effect rendered by a digital film service company called Cinesite, under the supervision of Micheal McAlister and Cinesite's Brad Kuen. Close-ups of the Smoker pilot and gunner were shot against greenscreen and composited with sky backgrounds that were filmed in Hawaii. The Mariner shinnies to the top of the mast, where he is promptly targeted by the pilot. As the Mariner lines up his spear, the pilot realizes his jeopardy and severs the line with a bullet, freeing both himself and the trimaran.

The bond between the Mariner and his passengers is strengthened later on, when a drifter approaches the trimaran looking for a trade. Part of the transaction involves Helen, and when the drifter offers the Mariner some priceless magazine pages—sealed inside a bottle like the Ark of the Covenant—for Helen's services, the Mariner agrees. As she reluctantly goes below with the drifter, he informs her that he plans to take Enola, as well. This is too much for the Mariner and he immediately calls off the trade, fighting the protesting drifter to the death. It is a transforming moment; the coldness that has served the Mariner so well has been tempered by humanity and, in defense of a helpless child, a reluctant hero is beginning to emerge.

With major crises temporarily attended to, more practical issues must be faced; they have been days at sea and Helen and Enola are hungry. The Mariner, goaded into action by Enola's innocent suggestion that perhaps he doesn't know how to fish, decides to take matters into his own hands and jumps into the water with a strange, two-headed harpoon gun. Almost immediately, an exotic thirty-foot "whalephin" fish leaps up from behind the Mariner and swallows him whole. All seems lost until, suddenly, the harpoon explodes from within the fish, freeing the Mariner and serving up a feast.

The whalephin fish effect was achieved through a combination of computer-generated visual effects supervised by Micheal McAlister and live-action special effects rigged on location by Marty Bresin and crew. "I had many, many conversations with Marty about the whalephin effect," McAlister recalled. "Our approach was that, since the whalephin was actually supposed to leap out of the water and swallow the Mariner, we needed to construct a real, practical esophagus. Marty and his crew came up

The underwater replica of Denver was made more real by the application of miniature detail, including furniture, refrigerators, and plumbing.

with something that looked a lot like an eighteen-foot-long windsock. It could be dragged by a boat underneath the surface of the water, and it looked just like the mouth of a fish. We rigged it so that Kevin Costner's stunt double, Norman Howell, was dragged behind the boat—with the camera placed just at the surface—and had the windsock 'leap' out of the water and swallow him. As the windsock came out of the water, it became the inside of the fish that was visible from the camera. The exterior of the fish and the lips in front were added later on as a three-dimensional computer graphics model by Rhythm and Hues, under the supervision of Bert Terreri."

Considerable interactive water effects were also contributed throughout the film by Cinesite. "We really pushed the envelope on this movie in terms of the interaction between miniatures, computer-generated creatures and water," observed McAlister. "It was really the first time I know of that computer tools have been used to this extent to solve what has traditionally and historically been a *tremendous* problem in visual effects. In fact, in the past any time you had to deal with water interaction within a frame, you usually redesigned the shot around the problems. But we knew the software was available, and the talent was there at Cinesite; it was really a question of elbow grease. With *Waterworld* we were very bold in our approach. We dealt with water interaction that was right in front of the camera, with no sleight of hand; it was just right there to be looked at and critiqued—and it ended up being very successful."

The driving force behind the *Waterworld* story is the search for Dryland—the legendary promised land no one is completely certain exists. The only clue is the mysterious tattoo/map that Enola has as a strange inheritance from long-forgotten parents. Having become Enola's adoptive mother, Helen is fiercely protective of this miraculous child, while understanding that she represents their only hope for a good and decent life. "Helen believes in Dryland," observed Tripplehorn. "And until it's proven that Dryland doesn't exist, she'll never give up hope. She has a really strong spirit and, as a mother, will do anything to save her child. She also wants a better way of life for her people because civilization as she knows it is dying."

The Deacon is seeking Dryland as well. He knows that Enola holds the key, and he and his followers are doing everything in their power to relieve Helen of her young charge. The Mariner, in the meantime, has plans of his own. Although he's beginning to form a bond with Enola and Helen, he has not yet allowed himself to feel affection for them, and he decides to cruise by a nearby slave colony that would be happy to lighten his load by a couple of females. As he approaches, however, he senses that something isn't quite right. He uses an underwater periscope—in an optical effect rendered by Cinesite—and spies several Smokers who have been lying in wait on jetskis just beneath the surface. Pete Romano captured the second-unit footage in Hawaii during early February in a relatively calm area south of Kona known as Cook's Cove. A special rig was built off the back of a tugboat and set to catapult the Smokers out of the water on cue. When released, they shot to the surface in a howling fury, wrapping the trimaran in a gill net.

The slave colony was an impressive set engineered by Ralph Kerr and the special effects department. The intricate floating structure rose thirty-five feet above water and was connected to a sturdy buoy that extended about twelve feet below. A large steel pipe was installed in the center for support and then structured to branch out like a tree. Nancy Haigh and her crew of set dressers followed with the appropriate accoutrements. "The slave colony was equipped with various elements that had been salvaged from the sea," said Haigh, "the kinds of things to suggest that there were twenty people living on it. We also included items like airplane parts and boat doors for set dressing—and to hide the Smokers who have strung up dead bodies and are using them like puppets. Most of the dressing was done while the set was next to the pier, but after it was towed out Kevin Reynolds realized that it needed some additional detail. We barged some more stuff out and went to work. It was much harder on the open sea because we had to go up and down eighteen narrow stairs—while the *set* was moving up and down, side to side, and in a circle." The dizzying sequence also proved challenging for the "dead bodies" that were, in fact, extras who spent their day bobbing on the ocean along with the set.

The Mariner, Helen, and Enola escape the perils of the slave colony—thanks to some fancy maneuvers that include the deployment of a spectacular spinnaker sail. At the same time the Deacon wounds the Mariner with a gunshot, which pumps a trail of blood into the water. Through his telescope the Deacon sees the Mariner collapse; bloodhoundlike tracker sharks are immediately released to hunt down the wounded hero. Both the spinnaker sail and

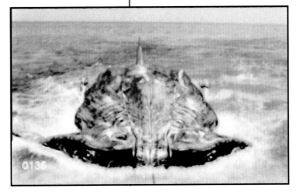

The whalephin fish was another mutated sea creature. Steve Burg envisioned it as having a mouth—packed with sharp teeth—that opened sideways.

tracker sharks were generated through three-dimensional computer animation by Rhythm and Hues.

While the Deacon goes about his nefarious business, Helen continues her campaign for Dryland. She knows the Mariner has access to the place because of the dirt he proffered for trade back at the atoll. She envisions the palm trees and flowers of Enola's drawings. Believing that Dryland is an ancient city long buried beneath the ocean, the Mariner agrees to take her there. The misunderstanding soon becomes clear when the Mariner takes Helen for an underwater sojourn in a diving bell and she discovers the true source of the precious soil—a park in the submerged city of Denver. The underwater dive was an ambitious sequence that represented an intensive, all-encompassing collaboration between the special effects and underwater photography departments.

Some of the footage establishing the diving bell was captured in Hawaii by Pete Romano, where a special effects rig was attached to the bell, pulling it down again and again to simulate its movement through the depths. The five-foot diving bell was designed and built by Peter Chesney and Image Engineering using flexible clear vinyl. Strips of eight-inch vinyl were glued over firmly sewed seams and a basketful of lead was placed beneath to pull the giant vinyl air bubble down to lower depths. A frame supporting a seat held Tripplehorn at waist-level out of the water. The ambient air inside the bubble was sufficient for about fifteen minutes, but oxygen from a scuba tank freshened the atmosphere from off camera. Air holes were installed on the side to release pressure and prevent the buoyancy from changing.

More extensive underwater footage of the diving bell was captured in December at McDonnell-Douglas—the aerospace corporation—where a large water tank was available. Typically used for astronaut weightlessness training, the seventy-foot wide, thirty-five-foot deep tank provided clear, filtered water in a meticulously controlled setting. Several weeks had been spent beforehand installing scaffolding, ladders, and an enormous thirty-foot underwater bluescreen, along with more than 120 underwater lights. As opposed to the footage filmed underwater in Hawaii, the McDonnell-Douglas shots were carefully designed to avoid having to propel the cumbersome prop at all. Instead, only the camera moved through the water, creating the illusion that the diving bell was descending toward the underwater city.

The bluescreen was used as a compositing tool to combine, during postproduction, the live-action footage with background plates of the miniature Denver that were shot separately by Stetson Visual Services. "The underwater bluescreen work was a very big deal," commented Romano. "Just the bluescreen alone, in terms of its size and the amount of light needed to backlight it, was beyond anything that had ever been put together. What made this shoot different from the other underwater scenes was that the bell and the actors remained stationary, while the camera made all the moves. For many of the shots, I was in a special harness being pulled back while holding my breath—I couldn't wear an air tank because of all the rigging I had to handle. I used a long snorkel to exhale so I wouldn't get air bubbles in the frame. At the same time, I was being buffeted by an air mover that was set off camera to cause a flow around the diving bell and to make Kevin Costner's hair move. We also had to contend with coordinating everything—the actors, the safety divers, the camera, the lights, the moves. It was tough. In all my years of shooting, this was some of the most complicated and difficult underwater photography I had ever done."

The tank work presented additional cinematic challenges, as well. Although the lighting considerations were immense,

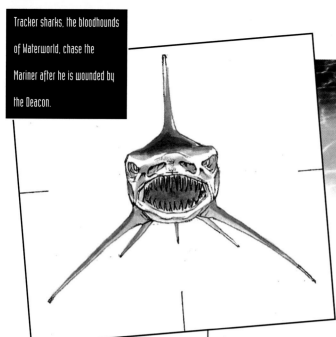

because of the lack of transmission through the blue-screen, the light levels remained relatively low. As a result, Romano had to shoot with his camera lens virtually wide open, resulting in a frustratingly limited depth of field. A further complication resulted from a particularly high chlorine content in the water—necessitated by an unexpected bloom of algae. "The close-up where the Mariner actually shows Helen the dirt was a very intense shot," recalled Romano. "It was the last shot that we did on the last day of filming and everybody was really tired. What made it harder was that I knew Kevin was in pain because of the chlorine level in the tank. It was clear that he was hurting, but he really hung in there. I think most people in a situation like that would say, 'Let me out of here!' But Kevin knew that this was important to the film. We got the shot just in time to break for the Christmas hiatus."

Construction of the miniature underwater city had begun months ear-

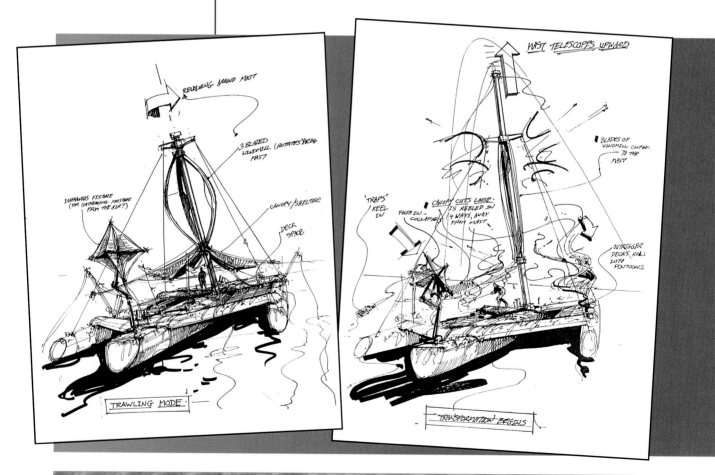

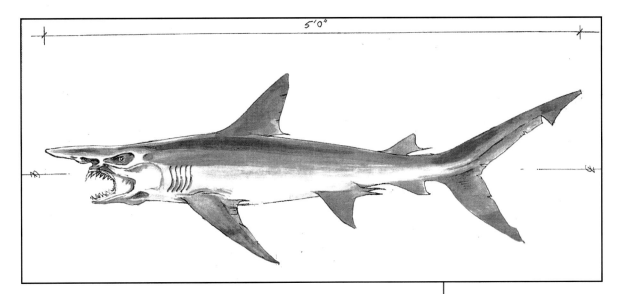

5'0"

lier at Stetson Visual Services under the supervision of Mark Stetson. Built primarily at twenty-fourth scale, Denver was conceived as a civilization long submerged hundreds of feet below the surface—and inaccessible to all but the Mariner. And although it would appear to be fathoms beneath the surface, the set was, in reality, shot on a sixty-by-eighty-foot sound

Steve Burg detailed the trimaran transformation sequence—from trawling to escape mode—in a series of sketches.

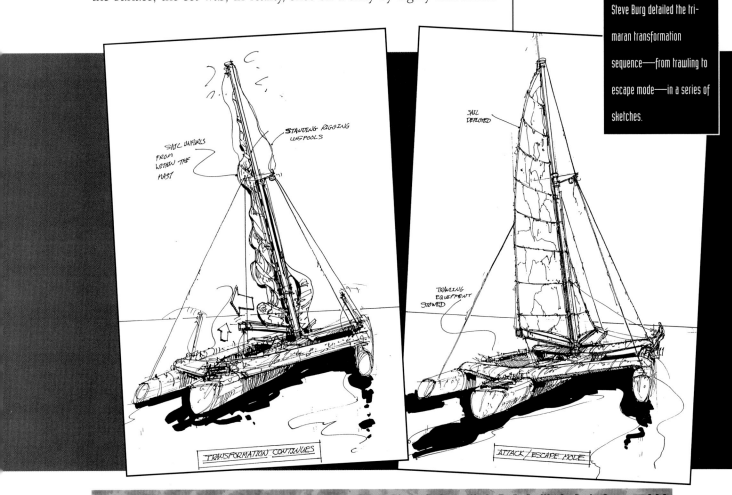

SAIL UNFURLS FROM WITHIN THE MAST

STANDING RIGGING UNSPOOLS

TRANSFORMATION CONTINUES

SAIL DEPLOYED

TRAWLING EQUIPMENT STOWED

ATTACK/ESCAPE MODE

stage with smoke pumped in to create the appropriate underwater atmosphere. "We used the classic dry-for-wet technique," explained Stetson, who also supervised the photography for the sequence. "The smoke was carefully monitored and metered so that it held a consistent density to simulate atmospheric degradation. The lighting was gelled blue and we occasionally used filters in the camera to complete the illusion of being underwater."

The depths of the city were somewhat abstract and certain conceptual compromises had been made in establishing the underwater reality. "There was a reference in the script to the city being a little more than 400 feet deep," observed Stetson, "while, in fact, the buildings of downtown Denver are upwards of 300 feet. We knew, in terms of the story, that we needed something more dramatic. There is a long sequence of shots leading down in depth to the city, so there's not too great a sensibility as to exactly how deep you are. Because of that, we were able to dress Denver a bit more prettily than you might find at the true depth of the city."

Stetson worked along with George Trimmer, who served as a consultant on the project, and crew chief Ian Hunter, who headed the crew responsible for building the highly detailed set. "The theory behind basing the city in Denver," explained Hunter, "was that, being the 'Mile High City,' it would be the highest city left as the world became covered with water. To reflect that, we built models that suggested a derelict city that had been submerged for several centuries. We looked at old shipwrecks for reference, and Mark Stetson is an avid diver—as were other people in the shop—so we had plenty of personal material to draw from." The model builders looked closely at images of the *Titanic* and Truk Lagoon, a location in Micronesia where a Japanese fleet was sunk during World War II, while determining the effects of long-term underwater corrosion.

Prior to constructing the enormous twenty-fourth scale model, a much smaller cardboard mock-up version had been devised. Based on storyboards established beforehand, the eight-by-eight-foot miniature was set up and shot on a smoke-filled stage using videotape. The sequence was then edited and sent to Hawaii, where the filmmakers, who were still deeply involved in first-unit photography, could critique it and return it for revision. This process continued for several months until the sequence was completely refined and the final set could be constructed to the precise needs of the film. Ultimately, eight twenty-fourth scale modular buildings were built. To create the illusion of a great metropolis, the various buildings were repositioned during filming, making it seem like there were many more structures than there actually were. Several larger twelfth-scale models were also built for use in the foreground.

Under ordinary circumstances, miniature buildings are typically fashioned from framed boxes with windows and other detailing added to complete the structural illusion. For the Denver set, however, such standard practices did not suffice. "We had to make the assumption that after centuries underwater, most of the glass, walls, and exteriors would have crumbled and disintegrated," said Hunter. "There would have been only fragments of structure left. Because of that, we had to create buildings that looked like big skeletons. George Trimmer and I came up with a system of using aluminum frames for the center of each building and then surrounding them with plastic I-beams and girders."

The skeleton sets were built on casters for easy maneuvering, and then textured with the same joint compound used on the walls of real houses. A similar technique was used to add rust and growth to the buildings to suggest an organic layer of marine growth. Hundreds of details were added to help sell the scale, including furniture, refrigerators, wall studs, and plumbing. "Everyone knows that wall studs, for example, are a certain size," noted Hunter. "Including such elements in the models really helps the audience identify the scale of the city. Those little items are subliminal, but if the eye catches them it registers in the brain and makes it all seem plausible. Without those details, the audience might subconsciously notice they're missing and get the feeling that something is not quite real about the scene. We didn't want that."

The dramatic emphasis of the sequence was underscored by the presence of an atomic submarine that had crashed in the middle of a major Denver boulevard. "The submarine was a particularly strong image that Steve Burg had come up with early in preproduction," Hunter continued. "It was the perfect way to indicate that nature had taken over man's best attempts at controlling water—that even this huge atomic submarine had failed and ended up crashing into the middle of the city." A twenty-foot submarine was rented for the production and carefully coated with liquid rubber latex. The vessel was then corrupted with barnacles, rust, and crumpled sheet metal—to indicate the damage that had occurred when it crashed—and then meticulously painted. After the shoot, the model crew stripped off the rubber and repainted the model.

"It was the perfect way to indicate that nature had taken over man's best attempts at controlling water—even this huge atomic submarine had failed and ended up crashing into the middle of the city."

Although Denver was ostensibly under more than 400 feet of water, it was determined that a shallower, tropical coral reef setting would be more aesthetically pleasing, while making better sense in terms of the Mariner's dive with Helen. Flocking guns, like the kind used to cover Christmas trees, were used to spray on a built-up organic crust. Small-scale sea anemones, coral, and crabs were added and flocked, as well. Generic details, provided by the model crew, further embellished the miniature set. "After building all these exacting models and getting very close to our work," said Hunter, "we started to back off a little bit and have some fun with the sequence. We knew that *Waterworld* was probably going to be the last major movie that Stetson Visual was going to do—since Mark Stetson and his partner, Robert Spurlock, had amicably decided to take different career paths—so, along the way, we decided to add some little homages to our past work. All through the dive sequence were things like the monolith from *2010* and the glider from *Escape From New York*. We included the orca from *Jaws* and the Bat Boat from *Batman Returns*. Since we were diving down *onto* the city, we saw a great deal of the roofs of the buildings, so we added helicopter pads and air conditioners and so on—but it was also convenient for us to include the helicopter from *Die Hard* and the spinner from *Blade Runner*. All these things were covered with flocking so there was no way they would read in the film, but we knew they were there. After spending ten or twelve hours a day on a project for months and months, it was a fun way to lighten things up a little."

Aside from the innovative application of miniature detail, color was another consideration. "We used a lot of color on this set to try and overcome the basic blue tone of the deep-water lighting," said Stetson. "It almost looked like the Disney submarine ride, it was so bright and vibrant. We used Day-Glo paint and primary colors in many places throughout the set but none of it came out—it still all looked blue. There were a few spots of color that happened to pop—if they got close enough to camera so that they weren't degraded by the blue light and smoke—that we had to paint back down. But mostly the image on film was quite monochromatic."

In addition to the underwater cityscape, Kevin Reynolds also wanted some neighboring mountains covered with ski slopes and an observatory to lend a sense of perspective to the scene. The Stetson Visual crew created a small mountain model out of rigid urethane foam that was sliced into contoured sections. The sections were then enlarged to about twenty times their original size, and a mountain was created from plywood, screen wire, and urethane foam. The sturdy construct provided a solid surface upon which crew members could climb to place miniature twigs and texture. Ski-lift pylons were built in diminished scale in order to compress space, with twenty chairs added in increasingly smaller sizes. A mechanism was attached to the final two chairs causing them to sway as if a current of water were gently flowing past.

The entire dive sequence was shot using a motion control camera by the director of photography for the sequence, Alex Funke. The motion control equipment allowed Funke to use, and consistently repeat, moves that lent a magical, fluid quality to the camera passes while creating a sensation of underwater weightlessness. Organic imperfections were added to the camera's flawless moves, thus loosening the mechanical smoothness of motion control and imbuing it with a realistic quality that integrated seamlessly with above-the-water footage.

The problem of underwater lighting was also addressed in a creative fashion. During the dive sequence, a flare attached to the diving bell lights the way after the Mariner and Helen have moved beyond the reaches of sunlight. To add a practical flare light to the miniature, tiny rigs were built on the tiny wires of high-intensity bulbs to shine on the models and create an interactive lighting effect as the diving bell passed through the scene. The flares helped indicate the depth of the action, while serving as a bridge between the live action and the model.

A miniature seabed was created from a combination of sand and vermiculite, with thin lines of colored pigment blown softly across the surface to suggest flow patterns that might have been created by the movement of the water. Live-action close-up shots were filmed with Costner and Tripplehorn in the McDonnell-Douglas tank to tie in with the miniature, where a heavier, claylike composition was derived to avoid muddying the clear water of the tank.

During postproduction, computer-generated air bubbles, flares, rope, and particles were added to the sequence to layer it with an indisputable sense of reality. "The dive sequence was as challenging a sequence as I've ever been associated with," commented Brad Kuen of Cinesite "It was a time where we could suspend the audience in a totally imaginary world. We had done some tests, and a lot of research, and discovered that in order to make it convincing that the characters were underwater, there needed to be a distinct interaction *with* the water. We added computer-generated particles into the water to show their interaction and it worked beautifully. The underwater sequence was the romantic part of the movie, and it stood alone all by itself. It didn't intercut between live action and effects—it was all effects work."

6. A VAST BLACK SHADOW

All the voyage of their life
Is bound in shallows and in miseries.
On such a full sea are we now afloat,
And we must take the current when it serves,
Or lose our ventures.

William Shakespeare

Somewhere beyond the endless blue horizon of Waterworld lies a different world. It exists not in the magical depths of an underwater city, nor in the imagined promise of foliage and firm ground. It is a darker place; a city of shadows bound by fog. Called the *'Deez,* it is, in reality, an ancient supertanker that serves as the Deacon's stronghold and home to his grim and grimy followers. As the Mariner and Helen emerge from their underwater journey, they are surprised by the Deacon and a handful of Smokers who steal Enola and hold her prisoner within the ironclad walls of this strange citadel.

The idea had first begun with Peter Rader, when he conceived of a supertanker as the ideal habitat for the story's oil-guzzling, environmentally incorrect antagonists. Later drafts of the script identified it more specifically: the Smokers' home was christened the *'Deez* after the infamous supertanker *Valdez* that dumped 240,000 barrels of oil into Prince William Sound when it ran aground in 1989. The accident had devastated the pristine waters rich in otters, whales, porpoises, seafowl, and fish—and marked the worst U.S. tanker spill in history.

The *'Deez* was the antithesis of the atoll in every way. Where the Atollers lived in an exquisite, albeit stark, balance with the elements, the Smokers seemed intent on pillaging resources beyond repair. While the Atollers understood the delicate relationship between population and the envi-

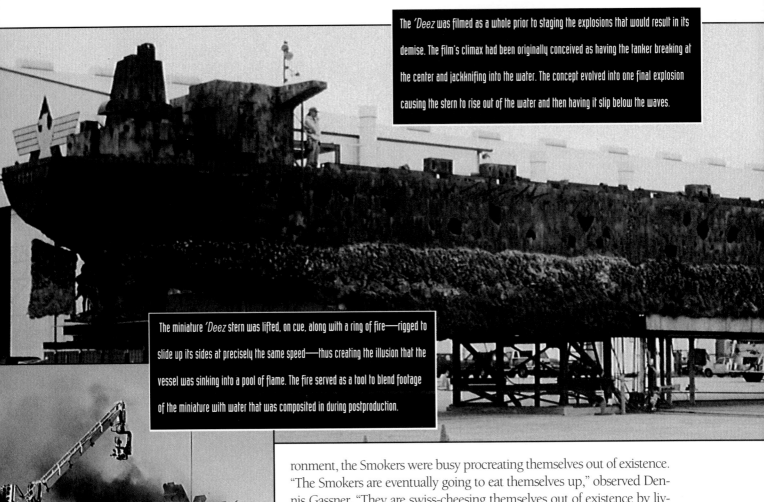

The 'Deez was filmed as a whole prior to staging the explosions that would result in its demise. The film's climax had been originally conceived as having the tanker breaking at the center and jackknifing into the water. The concept evolved into one final explosion causing the stern to rise out of the water and then having it slip below the waves.

The miniature 'Deez stern was lifted, on cue, along with a ring of fire—rigged to slide up its sides at precisely the same speed—thus creating the illusion that the vessel was sinking into a pool of flame. The fire served as a tool to blend footage of the miniature with water that was composited in during postproduction.

ronment, the Smokers were busy procreating themselves out of existence. "The Smokers are eventually going to eat themselves up," observed Dennis Gassner. "They are swiss-cheesing themselves out of existence by living on fossil fuel and, literally, cutting into the sides of their home to provide ammunition for their weapons. They consume canned meat, smoke cigarettes, and live on a supertanker. Obviously their world is going to reflect that. The Atollers, on the other hand, try to use the environment in a friendly way. They respect nature and use the forces of the wind. They stand in contrast to the Smokers—sort of like the guy who rides a mountain bike as compared to someone who drives a hot Ford with a 456 fuel-injected engine. This contrast was one of the things I liked about doing this movie—that if we don't watch our planet today and make wise choices, we could end up like the Smokers."

Coming up with a thousand-foot super oil tanker had posed one of the larger concerns the production company had initially faced. Purchasing such a vessel was considered in the beginning, but logistical and environmental issues had immediately ruled the idea out. Instead, the design and construction teams tackled the tremendous challenge of constructing massive interior and exterior sets of the 'Deez, while Stetson Visual Services built an impressive 112-foot miniature that would float, ultimately, in a sea of computer-generated water.

In August 1994, while first-unit efforts were under way on the atoll in Hawaii, construction crews had begun working on a 600-foot exterior of the supertanker's deck in a large field adjacent to the Pacific Tube Company in the City of Commerce. The location was chosen

because the outdoor lot could easily facilitate the large-scale set while providing an adjacent warehouse with plenty of space for interior sets. It was also considered ideal because it provided enough space for Craig Hoskins to land the Deacon's scout plane on its runwaylike surface—a plan that was later eschewed when it was determined that the plane could be more safely landed elsewhere. To this end, a separate stretch of *'Deez* runway was constructed in the Mojave Desert a few hours north of Los Angeles.

The 120-foot-wide-by-600-foot-long deck set was designed using forced perspective to create the illusion of the actual 900-foot deck of the supertanker *Valdez*. The forced-perspective section began about 200 feet from the bow of the ship, which meant that from the point of view of the superstructure at the stern—or rear—of the ship, the bow appeared to

extend to the full 900-foot length. In reality, however, that final section was actually built and painted at a smaller scale than the full-sized set, and diminished in size toward the vanishing point of the horizon.

The main part of the deck was built primarily of wood, both for ease of construction and durability during filming. The superstructure, which was built of wood and steel, required a more elaborate concrete foundation. Representing the tallest part of the tanker, the superstructure contained the pilot house, the engine room, the galley, the computer systems, quarters for the crew, and so on. The remainder of the ship below deck was, at least in theory, comprised of enormous baffles, or storage areas, that had at one time been used for the storage of oil. Holes were cut out of the deck and along the sides to suggest entry into the bowels of the ship. In Waterworld reality, the oil-coated baffles now yielded housing for thousands of Smokers.

Construction of the deck set was completed by mid-November, after which special effects crews descended on the structure to run the considerable plumbing required for the propane explosions, blasts, mortars, and firebombs that would be used during the final confrontation between the Deacon and Mariner. Sixteen propane tanks were set up along the sides of the 'Deez to supply adequate fuel for the event. By January, principal photography was ready to commence, with the visual effects department compositing the large-scale 'Deez exterior with background water plates during postproduction.

"The '*Deez* required a lot of choreography between units," noted McAlister. "We had to match the amount of smoke that emanated from the holes in the side of the ship, as well as the explosion that occurs at the end of the film, with miniature footage that was being shot elsewhere. We also had to deal with an oil tanker deck that was sitting in a dirt field surrounded by trees, telephone poles, airplanes, trains, and buildings. Nearly two-thirds of the shots taken at Commerce needed some sort of doctoring to get rid of those extraneous elements. As a result, we did a *lot* of wire "sky garbage" removals, where we borrowed imagery from the sky of some other portion of the frame and painted out the offending objects. It was all done through computer."

While the exterior set was being built, construction was also under way on the interior of the '*Deez.* Some of the interior sets had been con-

structed and filmed in the sugar shack at Kawaihae Harbor—most notably the Deacon's stateroom, the infirmary, the brig, the launch port, and a pulley system used to transport the Mariner through the different levels of the ship. Interiors were also built in the City of Commerce warehouse, which provided abundant area for "cover sets" that could be used as an alternative to the outdoor location in the event of inclement weather—a fortuitous circumstance that made filming possible during the devastating storms that struck Southern California in January 1995.

The largest interior set measured nearly 300 feet in length and depicted the segmented levels of the tanker. "It looked like catacombs as far as the eye could see," described David KIassen, "because, once again, we used forced perspective to make the set appear to go on and on. The idea was that since the Smokers use oil to run all their jetskis and gunboats, they cut the boat apart to expose the oil levels. They also use the metal for ammunition and weapons. So we made a lot of large holes and cut between beams of steel going down toward what were once the bulkheads. The set also had a very oily, filmy quality to the surface to depict dried oil." Painted plywood cutouts of Smokers were added in the background to enhance the overpopulated milieu, and ambient fires burned in bins and barrels. Hot shafts of sunlight—actually carefully placed camera lighting—poured through holes that had been cut in the walls and deck of the tanker to heighten the sense of reality.

Additional indoor sets included a forge, a refinery, and an oar room— for the scene in which the Smokers wield massive ironclad oars in an attempt to row the *'Deez* toward Dryland. A bluescreen-backed tanker bridge was built for when the Deacon presents a lengthy sermon and introduces Enola to his followers as the child who will lead them to the promised land. "The Deacon is a warrior priest," observed Dennis Hopper. "He's very similar to a lot of our world political leaders. He thinks it's better to be king than captain, and he refers to himself as the Deacon, I suppose, because of his religious-fanatic followers, who he rewards by giving them cigarettes. The Deacon is a humorous villain, but he's not likable in any way. He's actually

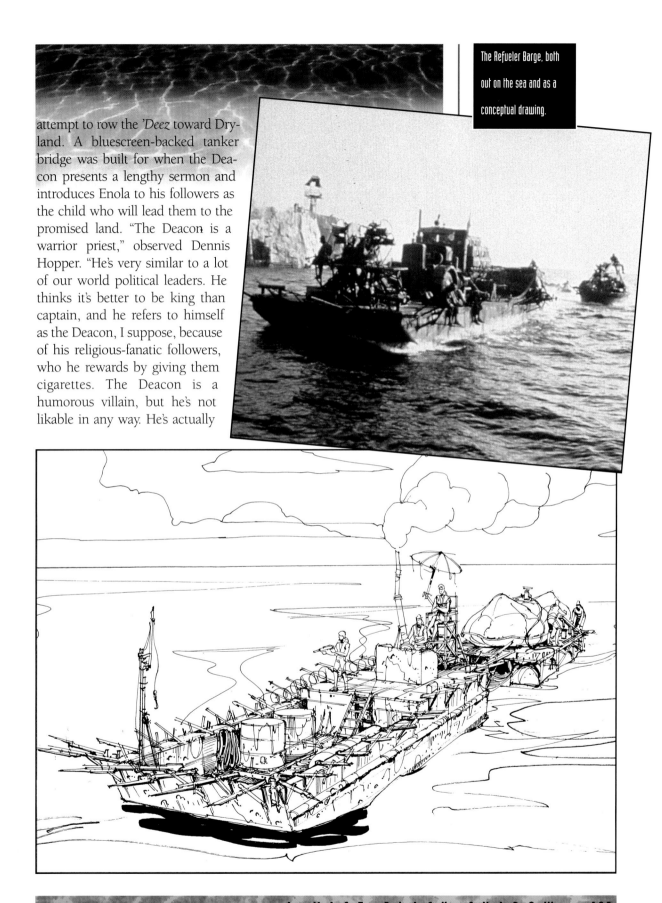

pretty detestable. He kills people like flies and doesn't have feelings for anyone, which makes him a very dangerous guy to be around. He wasn't really too complicated for me to play. I just had to get into a rhythm with him and then relax and bring it all down."

Both interior and exterior *'Deez* sets were dressed after construction teams completed their work. The deck was lined with large metal shipping containers, similar to the ones used to ship materials to Hawaii months earlier, that represented Smoker habitats. Hovels made of metal, cardboard, and plastic were also devised.

* * *

The Mariner has meanwhile discovered the 'Deez by tracking it in a unique way. After a couple of Smokers attack an atoll newly formed by Gregor and a few surviving Atollers, the Mariner dispatches the Smokers and commandeers their jet-skis. He then blows up one of the conveyances, which, in turn, ignites a line of oil that has been left on the surface of the water. Following the trail of flame, the Mariner rides the remaining jetski into the smoky fog that perpetually surrounds the 'Deez.

The Mariner's arrival at the 'Deez is marked by his confusion. After many centuries in the water, the 'Deez's hull has taken on a decidedly organic texture and its nature is, at first, unclear. But after he scrambles up the barnacled side and gets his bearings, the Mariner quickly ascertains his whereabouts in a sequence that was shot on location in Hawaii, on the 'Deez deck at the City of Commerce, and at an outdoor tank on the Paramount Pictures lot in Hollywood.

The Paramount tank footage was captured during the worst week of the January storm, causing considerable discomfort to the cast and crew and trying patience already tested by the lengthy and difficult shoot. Construction crews had raised a wooden wall that measured just over thirty feet in height to represent the base of the ancient vessel. Foam barnacles were then sculpted and coated with resin, to render them structurally sound, and painted the appropriate oil-saturated colors. The wall extended nearly 100 feet in length and rested in four and a half feet of water. "We had to anchor the wall quite substantially," said Klassen, "because, after all, wood and foam float. We used cables going up through the foam that were attached to

Dennis Hopper's interpretation of the warrior-priest leader was based on the notion that the character thought it was better to be king than captain. The Deacon's penchant for sermonizing helped earn him his name.

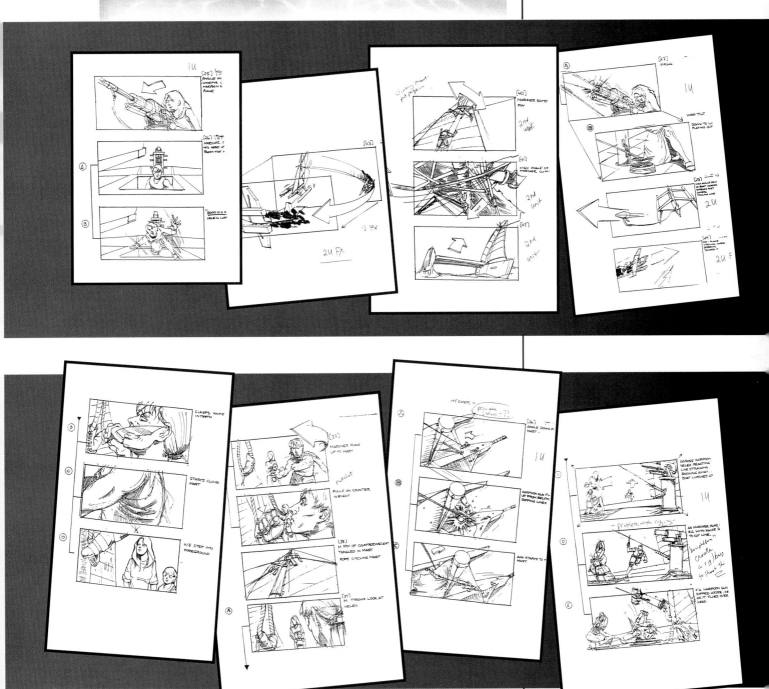

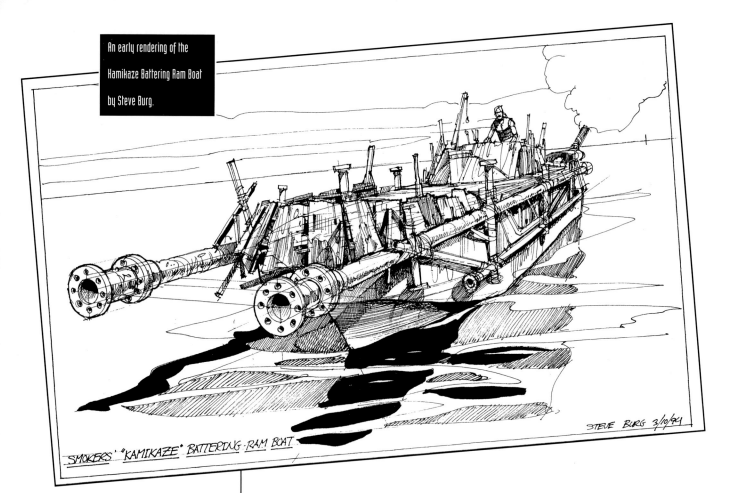

SMOKERS' "KAMIKAZE" BATTERING-RAM BOAT

STEVE BURG 3/10/94

buckets of concrete beneath. The whole thing was then anchored to a stair framing."

After Kevin Costner was filmed climbing up to the top of the structure, the camera was readjusted to face down to where a greenscreen had been positioned. A plate was later composited to create the illusion that the Mariner was looking ninety feet down from the deck of the 'Deez—as opposed to the relatively modest height of the wall.

Because of the rain, vast expanses of tarps were draped around the 140-foot tank in an attempt to shield the set, but enough water drained through to soak the wood and bubble the paint, thus requiring emergency repairs prior to filming. Fortunately, several days with only mildly overcast skies arrived in time to complete the shoot in comparative comfort.

In the film, the Mariner jumps from the deck of the 'Deez into the water between two Smokers who, clued in by his abandoned, blood-spattered jetski, are beginning to wonder exactly what is going on. He takes the pair underwater with him, kills them, and emerges wearing Smoker attire and goggles. Underwater footage for the sequence had been captured months earlier in Hawaii. "We were into a weather day and couldn't shoot on the ocean at all," recalled Romano, "so Dean Semler suggested we shoot in the harbor. I was skeptical because we only had about five feet of visibility, but Dean felt it would work because, being near the 'Deez, the water was *supposed* to be dirty. It ended up working out amazingly well. There wasn't much visibility, but we didn't need it because we were very

close to Kevin Costner and the stuntmen who played the Smokers. You could really see their features and grimaces as they were drowning, and we got some really good close-ups of Kevin grabbing their feet as they were kicking. It ended up being a very interesting sequence."

The Mariner then boards the 'Deez through the launch port and begins winding his way through multitudinous levels of steel and squalor. The Deacon's voice drones on through the tanker's public address system as he continues his sermon, while the Smokers realize an intruder is in their midst and begin to pursue the Mariner. As the Mariner nears the bridge, the Deacon—having worked himself into something of a frenzy—orders his followers to weigh anchor for Dryland. Momentum is gained when lengthy steel oars begin to stroke the water. Finally, the Mariner faces his enemy in a confrontation that culminates with a flare dropped down a calibrated shaft into an oil lake at the base of the tanker. A chain reaction of explosions begins rumbling through the various levels of the 'Deez.

Although large-scale sets were used for the deck and interiors, all reveals of the vessel were accomplished exclusively with a 112-foot miniature constructed in sections under the supervision of Robert Spurlock—along with crew chiefs John Stirber and Scott Schneider—in Stetson Visual's Los Angeles shop. The sections were then painstakingly loaded onto flatbed trucks and transported to an isolated airfield a few hours away in Mojave, California, where, remarkably, footage of the 'Deez was captured entirely within the desert setting.

Aside from matching the appearance of the Commerce set, the supertanker had to be capable of withstanding explosions and fire. It was also required, ultimately, to sink into the ocean wrapped in a ring of flames—in an effect that called for considerable rigging and logistical coordination.

"The unique thing about this sequence was that we were sinking a boat in the desert as if it were sinking in water," Spurlock observed. "Mike McAlister did a great job designing the shots so that when the miniature footage was combined with the ocean plates, it all looked absolutely real."

That reality began with designs inspired by the original *Valdez*. But while the artwork provided an excellent conceptual reference for the vessel, John Stirber and miniature designer George Trimmer required specific dimensions of the ship to accurately engineer a realistic model. While attempting to track down blueprints of the *Valdez*, they discovered that no public records remained available. Persistent detective work ultimately uncovered accurate dimensions of the ship's hull, and a tour of the *Valdez's* sister ship provided the model builders with an awe-inspiring sense of scope.

"We did a big research project trying to find information on the actual boat so George could start drawing," said modelmaker Ian Hunter, "but even after we tracked down the measurements, we still had another problem to face: the live-action set they were building in Commerce was built at a diminished scale and wasn't an accurate portrayal of the actual *Valdez*. The Commerce set was narrower at the front and back, and if we had built our boat to those proportions, it would have ended up looking pretty silly."

The climactic battle on board the *'Deez* was staged on location at the City of Commerce where a large-scale deck set had been constructed in the middle of an open field. Scores of extras were hired for the sequence.

So the miniature '*Deez* ended up being a cross between the actual *Valdez* dimensions and the set that was built in Commerce."

The '*Deez* miniature was built at one-eighth the scale of the full-sized tanker when it was determined that the proportions of water and flames appeared the most realistic at this size. "Eighth scale meant three and a half inches to the foot of the regular ship," elaborated John Stirber. "We built the model in ten-foot sections and included an enormous amount of rigging. We added fire-injection systems, electrical igniting systems, air systems, and fan backups for when we used small explosions, as well as air mortars for burning debris. We did a lot of tests to determine the look of the fire. For the miniature, we had to intensify the flame movement so that it moved four or five times faster than what seems real to the eye. That way, when it ran at normal speed, the fire conveyed a realistic sense of scale." A steel frame structure was built and covered with eighth-inch luan, after which crews affixed very thin steel panels that would serve, primarily, as fire protection. Fireproof boxes were factored into the construction so that flames could be safely ignited and extinguished for repeated takes.

Four separate superstructures were also built. A hero structure—the one intended to read most authentically on film—was made of plywood and used for all the beauty shots of the '*Deez*. Three balsa wood models

The demise of the 'Deez required months of advance preparation. The steel-framed tanker miniature was carefully fireproofed, and equipped with fire injection systems and air mortars to blow up on cue under the supervision of crew chief John Stirber.

were also built and laced with primer cord and gas mortars to blow up on cue. "We had to match all four superstructures so the paint jobs were identical, along with the texture and details," noted Scott Schneider. "We covered all the balsa wood with black wrap foil, so that when it blew up, you didn't just see the balsa wood, you could definitely see foil tearing and it didn't look so woody. One of the funny things about the balsa wood superstructures, though, was that we couldn't put them together with screws—that would have read on camera and thrown the scale complete-ly off. So we glued them together and covered the weld lines with spaghet-ti—because spaghetti will shatter—and then textured over that."

As they had with the underwater city, model crews embellished the miniature 'Deez with meticulous detailing that rendered it unquestionably authentic. Schneider and Hunter made frequent trips to the Commerce set during the construction and set-dressing phases to take reference pho-tographs. That way, they were able to match detail so that footage intercut between the miniature and full-scale sets would be indistinguishable.

"Over time we managed to get everything pretty close," said Schneider. "We made habitat containers in various sizes to match the ones on the full-scale set. We added things like miniature antennas, bedsprings, ladders, couches, car seats, and so on. We also included holes in the decks and along the sides. Modelmaker Adam Gelbart even built two eighth-scale Helio Couriers—one for a crashed plane and one for a hero plane—although we ended up only using the hero plane, which sat on the deck for a lot of the fire shots."

To enhance the authenticity of the scale, dozens of nautical items were also included. "We cast a lot of things you would typically find on a ship," noted Trimmer, "and that really helped sell the scale. We made miniature door portals, window portals, handrails, stairs, fifty-five gallon drums—things that were easily recognizable. We even hand-built a lot of the handrails out of real metal." The 'Deez's fortresslike appearance was accentuated with miniature I-beams that formed a thorny crown along the perimeter of the deck.

The miniature deck was further garnished with twelfth-scale Smoker bodies to represent the carnage resulting from the explosions. Four different Smoker types were sculpted out of clay and then made into plaster molds from which latex rubber and polyfoam puppets were cast. About ten puppets were cast from each of the different molds, resulting in a total of forty Smoker puppets. Some were fitted with flexible armatures so they could be posed, others had lead in their feet and hands so that, during the explosion, they tumbled like real bodies. Puppets that came out of the cast less than perfect were covered with blood and scattered across the deck as dead bodies. During the live-action 'Deez shoot in Commerce, hundreds of extras had served as full-scale Smokers for the battle sequence, in footage that was effectively intercut with the miniature.

The miniature's hull was encased with barnacles and coral to suggest many centuries of waterlogged degradation. Flexible polyester barnacle panels lined the hull of the tanker at the waterline and were textured with

Kevin Costner as the Mariner with producer Charles Gordon.

spray-on foam. Once the model was completed, painter Ron Gress covered it with the appropriate hues. "Repainting the model was an essential step in the process," commented Spurlock. "We spent about ninety percent of our efforts making the model and perhaps five percent on the paint

job—but most of the look came through the paint. You can have a wonderful shape and texture, but if it isn't painted right, the whole thing is going to look bad. Ron Gress did a tremendous job on the 'Deez; he really set the tone for us."

The task of filming the miniature fell to director of photography for the 'Deez unit, Mark Vargo, who began shooting in January. "The main objective was to make the tanker look big," he noted. "After all, it was supposed to be 1,000 feet long. We chose Primo lenses to avoid any foreshortening of the image, and selected angles to help create the sense of enormity. I didn't realize how big a supertanker was until I actually visited the Arco *Independence* in Long Beach. It was a *huge* vessel. I tried to guarantee that the ship looked great in flattering light, but that it also looked immense. Logistically and operationally, shooting the *'Deez* was a very complicated piece of business."

Part of Vargo's job also involved matching the miniature photography with first- and second-unit footage shot in Hawaii. To accomplish this, the model was aligned to the same compass heading as the set in Commerce. Vargo emulated Semler's lighting scheme by making sure the miniature was lit from the front and side. "The mandate was to shoot under clear, sunny skies," said Vargo, "and I preferred to shoot later in the afternoon when the side of the ship was shadowed, but the superstructure was illuminated, just to give it a little bit more scale."

The water surrounding both the miniature *'Deez* and the live-action set was generated by Cinesite and composited into the footage during postproduction. "We knew from the beginning we were going to have to add water to the miniature," said Brad Kuen, "but we went through a process of testing and exploration before we figured out exactly how to do it. Mike McAlister had talked about the problem of matching scale between the 600-foot deck and the 112-foot miniature; we needed to be sure we could intercut the water between the two *and* get plates of the *'Deez* to marry with plates of the water. That was a real challenge. In the meantime we were working with a company called Arete that was doing some water simulation tests for the government. They did four tests involving different levels of water detail that gave us an idea of processing times. The last test blew everyone away; it was then that we knew the computer-generated water was going to work."

In the film, the explosions that progress through the *'Deez* culminate in a final, massive explosion that sends it sinking in a spectacular ring of flame. The climax had originally been conceived as having the *'Deez* breaking at the center and jackknifing into the water because of the stress —a genuine possibility with such a structure. Because of this, the model was designed to separate at the center into two major sections. The concept evolved, however, into having one final explosion causing the stern to rise out of the water and then slip below the waves, surrounded by fire.

To accomplish this, a 100-ton crane lifted the 16,000-pound stern section high off the ground while, at the same time, a ring of fire was rigged to slide up the sides of the doomed vessel at precisely the same speed. "The ring of fire was on a dual track system that had about forty-eight separate burning bars, which were mounted on a track that went through a cable system within the ship," explained Stirber. "A counterweight system connected the cables to a

winch, which made it easy to move. It was all tied into a computer on the camera, so that as the camera moved, the system that moved the ring of fire moved in unison, thus creating the illusion that the ship is sinking into the ocean surrounded by flames fueled by an oil slick." The extensive pyrotechnics were carefully choreographed by Roy Downey and crew, with safety personnel stationed off camera in the event of a mishap.

Computer-generated water was added to the footage during postproduction. "The one thing we wanted to avoid was actually putting water directly next to the miniature," said Kuen. "By putting *fire* around it we didn't have to worry about creating a waterline against the boat, which would have been almost impossible to integrate. There were a few other shots in the movie where the water had to hit the boat and come back, but we were able to avoid that problem for the final 'Deez sequence. With the digital technology now available it's possible to do almost anything—but that also creates a new set of problems. It was just a matter of putting a research team on it." For the final shot of the stern submerging into the water, a ten-foot section was filmed as it was lowered into a twenty-foot pool of water that had been dug at the Mojave site. The pool contained enough water area to frame a shot of the stern sinking and slipping below the waves, thus eliminating the need for computer-generated interaction of boat and waves.

As the 'Deez goes down, Gregor and Helen—along with the Enforcer from the atoll, played by R.D. Call—arrive with an armored version of Gregor's original escape balloon just in time to rescue the Mariner and Enola. The Mariner and company make their escape as the Deacon, who has boarded a jetski in a final, frantic attempt to grab Enola, crashes and dies.

Like the 'Deez, the balloon was a miniature that never existed as a full-scale set. A full-scale gondola was lifted by a crane and shot against blue-screen whenever close shots of the actors were required. Other than that, Gregor's dirigible was, in reality, a computer-generated model created by Boss Film Studios. The CG balloon was then connected to the practical gondola with computer-generated cables and ropes.

7. PROMISED LAND

Hence in a season of calm weather
Though inland far we be,
Our souls have sight of that
immortal sea
Which brought us hither.
William Wordsworth

Even Ulysses made it home in the end.

After generations afloat, and a legacy of Waterworld from time beyond memory, the Mariner and the embattled Atollers finally come ashore. It is overwhelmingly evident that Enola's artistic vision was true; Dryland is revealed as a place of exceptional beauty and wonders that had, heretofore, only been dreamed of. The party climbs out of the gondola and begins discovering the miracles of fresh water and tropical foliage—along with the village that bears the truth of Enola's heritage. The skeletal remains of her parents are found entwined on a cot within her family's hut next to a picture of Enola's tattoo.

Although it represents the final scene of the film, footage of Dryland was captured in September while the company was filming on location in Hawaii. The mythical promised land was set in one of the most sacred places in all the islands, the lush Waipio Valley on the eastern side of the Big Island. The September filming schedule was dictated by the imperative to beat the tropical rainy season that was expected by October. Oversized trucks were strictly forbidden, and crew members carried in sets and equipment using smaller, four-wheel-drive vehicles. After the three-day shoot, the area was respectfully returned to its original state.

The village set was comprised of four huts and dressed to suggest a combination of Polynesian and Nepalese influences. "Decor for the huts was based on research about Mount Everest and the trails for Katmandu," explained Nancy Haigh. "When people go on treks up the mountain, they stay in huts that have stone bases. We wanted to show that, over time, this mountainous area had become a tropical paradise with palm trees and reeds, so we built our huts with stone bases and added thatched roofs to reflect that. In addition to the Polynesian and Nepalese overtones, we wanted to include the idea that a society, even over five hundred years, would have passed on religious beliefs. We used some symbols from Buddhism and Hinduism to convey that. Cobwebs were then spread over everything. It was a very beautiful scene."

Haigh and crew also added an assortment of exterior flowers, birds, and vines to enhance the setting. Wild pigs and miniature horses, indigenous to the area, wandered across camera at will. The Edenlike locale even included a 300-foot waterfall that could literally be turned on and off on cue. Sluice gates controlled an irrigation system that permitted Kevin Reynolds to call forth a flood at precisely the right moment.

The film concludes with the Mariner saying good-bye to the Atollers—now Drylanders—and returning to the sea. Truly a creature born of Waterworld, he realizes he cannot stay on land and sets out in a boat he has discovered near the beach. Before he departs, each of the Mariner's friends gives him a gift. From Enola, he receives a music box; Gregor hands him a bag full of dirt; and the Enforcer extends the hand of friendship. Helen's gift is different and achingly precious—she gives the Mariner a name. He sails off and, as they watch his image growing smaller in the distance, Helen tells Enola the story of another warrior who drifted on the seas, and who—like the Mariner—was also called Ulysses.

Although *Waterworld* ended with the idyllic Dryland sequence, principal photography did not conclude until February 14, 1995—exactly one year to the day from the delivery of the French-built trimarans to the Kona Coast of Hawaii. It had been an intensive and frequently exhausting eight-month journey. The filmmakers had embarked on a quest to realize their unique vision and, in doing so, had squared off with Mother Nature, conventional filmmaking practices, and—all too often—a media that seemed intent on shining a dark light on the expensive and challenging production. Understandably, reports of budgetary excesses and scheduling delays exacted a toll on morale. "After a while it got to be a bit depressing," admitted Kevin Reynolds, "because there was so much negative press. But we tried not to let it get us down. At a certain point we realized we had a choice. Either we could become so defensive that we were constantly trying to refute the claims that these people are making—because they were, for the most part, pretty uninformed—or we could figure that it just wasn't worth it, and know that it was all going to blow over. We just put our heads down and made the movie because that was all we could do."

For Charles Gordon, the unwarranted media attention became a catalyst for excellence. "In a way, it became easier to carry on because the publicity rallied everybody," he said. "It actually served to bring the company together. Of course, it was tough psychologically waking up every morning to find another article about our movie that was, I would say, fifty percent inaccurate. That part was very dif-

An early concept rendering of Gregor seated in one of his myriad inventions—a Jules Verne-inspired flying machine.

ficult. But we were all professionals and knew there was only one way to quiet the press—to make a great movie and have it be successful. We knew from day one that it was going to be rough because we were doing something that had never been done before."

A twenty-week postproduction period followed immediately on the heels of principal photography, during which Reynolds turned his attention to the immediate matter of editing the film. He had worked throughout the production with film editor Peter Boyle, beginning in an editing room not far from Kawaihae Harbor. By the time the final edit was ready to commence in Los Angeles, considerable footage had already been ordered and assembled. Boyle had worked previously with Reynolds on *The Beast, Robin Hood: Prince of Thieves,* and *Rapa Nui,* as well as serving in like capacity on other

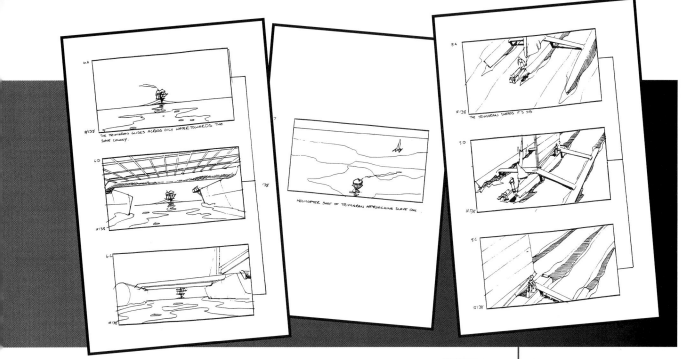

films, including *Sommersby* and *Into the West,* and came to the production with prior understanding of Reynolds's cinematic style.

For *Waterworld,* Reynolds and Boyle used a new computer digitized editing system called Lightworks—as opposed to the traditional method of splicing and taping film together—that proved highly expedient. "It has actually been quite amazing how much faster we can work using Lightworks as opposed to using film," commented Reynolds. "It still has a few software and programming glitches, but it cut the amount of time we required to look at various cuts by half. It is an amazing system. Neither Peter nor I had worked with it before, but Peter became very adept after using it for so many months. It really helped us keep track of footage more

efficiently—with a couple of keystrokes we could look at a take instead of having to file through a whole roll of film."

While editing represented one area of postproduction, sound for the film was another matter. Reynolds charged sound designer Jay Wilkinson with the task of making *Waterworld*'s dialogue audible over the relentless roar of the ocean and the endless intrusion of motorboats that affected the sound quality during filming. Extensive looping, or dubbing of dialogue onto the soundtrack under studio conditions, was clearly a necessity. "I've known Jay for a long time," said Reynolds, "and I think he's the best around. I had to give him very few notes as to what I wanted because his sensibility was so great that I trusted him implicitly to do whatever the scene called for." Wilkinson also made sure explosions raged at the appropriate pitch, and countless ambient noises were added to the soundtrack to enhance the story's realism.

The film's impressive score was composed by Mark Isham, who had recently provided orchestration for such films as *Losing Isaiah, Mrs. Parker and the Vicious Circle, Quiz Show, Shortcuts, Romeo Is Bleeding, Made in America*, and an Academy Award for *A River Runs Through It*—as well as having scored Reynolds's 1988 release, *The Beast*. "On a picture like *Waterworld* we needed big, expansive movie music that pushed all the right buttons and got people excited and emotional," commented Reynolds. "What I like about Mark is that he was able to accomplish that in a very unique way. I wanted someone who could come in with an unusual perspective and incorporate a lot of strange and unusual instrumentation to the music to make it truly original. The whole picture is about a world made up of the vestiges of many different yet familiar cultures that had all been mixed together in a big cosmic blender. I wanted the music to reflect sounds that seemed unique to a culture, but that might have gone through two or three

"The whole picture is about a world made up of the vestiges of many different yet familiar cultures that had all been mixed together in a big cosmic blender."

Although initially resistant, the Mariner eventually forms an affectionate—and enduring—bond with the child, Enola. Here he teaches her how to swim.

different incarnations over time. It was important for the music to have an amorphous, but at the same time, exotic sound. Mark also included a lot of water elements to give the music a very fluid, liquid quality."

Waterworld's premiere marked the culmination of a production that, in many ways, would stand alone in terms of cinematic ambition and achievement. Never before had such innovative sets been engineered to withstand open ocean filming; never before had underwater photography and visual effects been orchestrated to such a fervent degree. The sheer scope of the production—from props to costumes to crew—had made it an epic in every way. Yet despite the enormity of their endeavor, the filmmakers' ultimate goal had remained remarkably simple: to create a first-rate motion picture experience. "We wanted audiences to come away feeling entertained," said Gordon. "We wanted them to come away feeling that they got their money's worth and, hopefully, that they'd like to go see the movie again. That's really all we ever hope."

For Kevin Reynolds, *Waterworld* represented a once-in-a-lifetime experience. "*Waterworld* was cumbersome to make because it was so big; just trying to shape all the different elements and keep it moving in a certain direction was really tough. Dozens of variables had to be dealt with every day, and although I knew—at least intellectually—what I would be confronted with going in, it wasn't until I was involved that I understood what that truly meant. But I was committed to the process, and it became a matter of taking things as they came on a day-to-day basis. Making *Waterworld* was a great ride, and I wouldn't trade the experience for anything."